MUSCLE SHOALS

LOW RHYTHM RISING

FOREWORD BY JASON ISBELL

COUNTRY MUSIC FOUNDATION PRESS

222 REP. JOHN LEWIS WAY S • NASHVILLE, TENNESSEE 37203

Published 2025. Printed in the United States of America.

978-0-915608-50-8

This publication was created by the staff of the Country Music Hall of Fame® and Museum.

Editor: RJ Smith · Artifact photos by Bob Delevante · Printer: Jostens, Clarksville, Tennessee

PRINTED IN THE U.S.A. USING SOY-BASED INKS ON ECO-FRIENDLY PAPER

CONTENTS

FROM LEFT: Marvell Thomas, Etta James, and David Hood at FAME Recording Studio, August 1967. At the session produced by Rick Hall, James recorded "Tell Mama."

PHOTO COURTESY OF DAVID HOOD

DEAR MUSEUM FRIEND,

Muscle Shoals is only 125 miles from Nashville, but it might as well be the moon.

There are four Alabama towns—Muscle Shoals, Florence, Sheffield, and Tuscumbia—which cluster together along the Tennessee River and make room for a population that's barely a fifth of Nashville's. The pace is slow. The land is close to your feet. And life is quiet. Except when it comes to music.

Over the last sixty years, Muscle Shoals has earned its reputation as a small town with a gigantic voice. Here at the Museum, we've wanted to tell the Shoals story for a long time, but to tell it right we couldn't do it by ourselves. We needed the folks who made the story—the otherworldly creatives who live and breathe its music. So I got in the car with Michael Gray, the Museum's VP of Museum Services, and together we drove down there.

What we discovered was a proud and passionate community that offered us the kind of blessing that only natives have the power to bestow.

Rick Hall's son Rodney met us at FAME Studio. Room by room, we walked across sacred ground, and Rodney pledged his support on the spot. We were off to a good start.

Later on, we toured the Alabama Music Hall of Fame and the Muscle Shoals Sound Studio, where we received more enthusiastic, unequivocal interest. Veteran publicist and artist manager Traci Thomas even cooked supper for us.

We sat around her table and gleaned invaluable insight into the layered history of the Shoals—a complex narrative that features a varied cast of contributors.

Before we left town, much of that cast came together to lend us their listening ears, generous encouragement, and humbling support.

Plenty of work was left to do, but thanks to the kindness of community, Michael and I returned to Nashville with everything we needed to tell a story that everybody needed to hear.

Dan Penn is known for his hit songwriting and his trademark overalls.

ARTIFACT COURTESY OF DAN PENN

Our exhibit is called *Muscle Shoals: Low Rhythm Rising*. It traces the path of musicians—Black and white—who bridged segregation, forged unlikely alliances, and released to the world a brave new sound. And that new sound was like a beacon of soulful light, drawing a wide range of artists to claim their own portion of Alabama grit and soul. Geniuses like Aretha Franklin, Wilson Pickett, Bobbie Gentry, Willie Nelson, the Rolling Stones, Etta James, Bob Seger, the Staple Singers, Paul Simon, Cher, Traffic, Hank Williams Jr., and a whole lot more.

There's no doubt that music is the star of the exhibit, but that's not the whole story. *Muscle Shoals: Low Rhythm Rising* is about American perseverance, collaboration, and creativity, presented with scholarly depth and curatorial discernment.

Since you already know the music, allow us to introduce you to the place and its people.

Kyle

Kyle Young | CEO

ACKNOWLEDGMENTS

This book, and the exhibition it accompanies, benefited from the collaborative enthusiasm we encountered among many generous people in Muscle Shoals and Nashville.

In 2011, the Country Music Hall of Fame and Museum planted seeds for this project when it partnered with the Americana Music Association to present the panel discussion *Land of 1000 Dances: The Groundbreaking Sounds of Muscle Shoals*. Moderator Holly George-Warren solicited stories and insights from David Briggs, Donnie Fritts, Rick Hall, Jimmy Johnson, Dan Penn, Norbert Putnam, Spooner Oldham, and Candi Staton.

We are grateful to them and others who have allowed the museum to document the music of Muscle Shoals through our public programs over the decades. Briggs, Putnam, Jerry Carrigan, Mac McAnally, and David Hood have been featured in the museum's long-running series *Nashville Cats*, which spotlights musicians who have made significant contributions to roots music. Likewise, we interviewed Penn and Roger Murrah for *Poets and Prophets*, our ongoing series that honors legendary songwriters.

The museum invited Jason Isbell to be its 2017 Artist-in-Residence. In 2025, he generously volunteered his time to us again, sharing vivid memories and keen perspectives about Muscle Shoals that inform the book and the exhibit alike.

In the wake of FAME Studio founder Rick Hall's death in 2018, his family assisted us greatly throughout the development of the exhibit. Wife Linda Hall and Rodney Hall—one of Rick and Linda's three sons, and the president of FAME Publishing and FAME Records—gathered a treasure trove of artifacts and archival materials for us to use. They also welcomed us to film several interviews inside their historic studio. Additionally, Linda and Rodney agreed to be formally interviewed themselves and introduced museum staff to those in the community who figure prominently in the Muscle Shoals story. Mark Hall, another son of Rick and Linda, helped as well.

We are deeply indebted to legendary bassist David Hood and his wife, Judy. They met with us multiple times at Muscle Shoals Sound Studio, the studio David opened in 1969 with his fellow Swampers. David graciously sat down with our curators and film crew there; loaned us artifacts from his personal collection; and, with Judy, encouraged the Shoals community to support our efforts. David's son Patterson Hood—frontman for the Drive-By Truckers—also assisted us greatly throughout the development of the exhibit.

Several people graciously welcomed us into their homes, to share their stories and, in many cases, entrust us with personal materials for us to include in the book and exhibit. Among them were Dan and Linda Penn, Mickey and Beverly Buckins,

Norbert and Sheryl Putnam, Traci Thomas and Alan Daigre, Lise Davis (wife of the late Mac Davis), and Marlin Greene.

Throughout the project, we called upon Traci Thomas and Andreas Werner time and time again for guidance.

Many folks generously volunteered their time for oral history video interviews, including Mickey Buckins, Dick Cooper, Linda Hall, Rodney Hall, David Hood, Patterson Hood, Jimmy Hughes, Jason Isbell, Clayton Ivey, Bettye LaVette, Mac McAnally, Peanutt Montgomery, Spooner Oldham, Dan Penn, Norbert Putnam, the Secret Sisters (Laura Rogers and Lydia Slagle), the Shoals Sisters (Marie Tomlinson Lewey and Cindy Richardson Walker), Candi Staton, Swamp Dogg, Travis Wammack, and John Paul White.

Mark Beckett, Al Cartee. Kevin Lamb, Billy Lawson, Brian McGee, Jerry Phillips, and Richard Younger supplied us artifacts and photographs. Likewise, we are grateful to the Rock & Roll Hall of Fame, the Alabama Music Hall of Fame, the Leighton Museum, the Florence-Lauderdale Public Library, and the Alabama Department of Archives and History for helping us procure significant materials.

Music historian Rob Bowman assisted us greatly by writing copy for the exhibit interactives.

We also enlisted the help of Johnny Belew, Kissy Black, Debbie Bradford, John Briggs, Sandra Burroughs, Cassandra Hightower, Charles Holloman, Tonya Holly, Ana Hyde, TK Kimbrell, Will McFarlane, Ed McNees, Victoria Mitchell, Haley Phillips, Bridger Simons, Mike Smyth, Ben Tanner, and Debbie Wilson.

Many museum staff members devoted time and talent to the book and the exhibit. Space prohibits listing them all, but some deserve special mention here. Vice President of Museum Services Michael Gray co-curated the exhibit with RJ Smith and led the curatorial team that included Vice President of Creative Warren Denney, Executive Director of Exhibits and Curatorial Services John Sloboda, Mick Buck, Kathleen Boyle, Tori Hinshaw, Michael Manning, Shepherd Alligood, Kevin Fleming, Elek Horvath, Rosemary Zlokas, Jack Clutter, and Julea Thomerson.

Executive Vice President of External Affairs Lisa Purcell, Senior Director of Editorial Paul Kingsbury, Creative Design Director Bret Pelizzari, Senior Director of Creative Luke Wiget, Senior Graphic Designer Mills F.H. Penticoff, Senior Graphic Designer Roger Blanton, Director of Creative Project Management Sydney Gilbert, Associate Director of Creative Project Management Tess Pardee, and Senior Production Manager Whitney Waddell merit special recognition.

FINDING THE MAGIC

FOREWORD BY JASON ISBELL

Growing up in Alabama, I can't recall not having music as a foundational part of my life.

My extended family all played and sang—mostly gospel music and old hillbilly music. I was probably three years old when my parents would take me to my uncle's cover band practices, which would be in Danny Burnett's garage. I would fall asleep on the weightlifting bench while they were playing.

I knew from a very early age that there was a lot of great music that had been made right down the street in the Shoals. Just twenty miles south of where I grew up in Green Hill. But in Green Hill it was just a bunch of poor white kids. Listening to the music that had been made in Muscle Shoals was really the first experience that I had with the inner life of people who didn't look exactly like me. If that hadn't happened, I could have been a totally different type of person than I am now.

In the late sixties and early seventies in North Alabama, there was a bubble happening in the music scene, where people of all different kinds could work together and get along in the same places.

The system that was set up for the production of those records didn't favor everybody equally, but the finished product is a different story. I think the reach of the music itself can sometimes work to untangle the complications of how the music got made, and who benefited from it.

Listen to "When a Man Loves a Woman," and try to find something else that puts you in a very specific location and time so quickly and so easily. You just vanish from whatever seat you're in, and you go wherever Percy Sledge wanted you to go.

I fell so deeply in love with the Staple Singers' music, and Aretha Franklin's, and Wilson Pickett's, and Candi Staton's. I really, really studied, and listened over and over.

In the Shoals area, you couldn't have bars, really. You'd get shut down if you didn't sell more food than alcohol, which

Jason Isbell on the shore of Percy Priest Lake, Nashville, 2013. PHOTO COURTESY OF DAVID MCCLISTER

was difficult for any kind of live music scene—but it was great for a fifteen-year-old kid, because then they couldn't kick me out for being underage.

I would go listen to David Hood, Donnie Fritts, Barry Billings, Kelvin Holly, Mike Dillon, NC Thurman, Scott Boyer, Spooner Oldham, and on the rare occasion that Dan Penn would come out and play somewhere, I'd go see Dan. I followed those guys around, tried to learn how they played, and stole guitar licks from them.

David Hood was family to me—he called me "son." I would ask him, "How do you do it? How do you get to the place where you are as a musician?" And he would give me advice like, "Show up on time and make sure all your gear works."

That's not what I was looking for. What I was asking was, "What's the magic?" And the magic is: show up on time and make sure all your gear works.

I thought, "When I reach a certain age, I'm going to drive myself to FAME Studios." That's what happened. I made a demo with some friends, took it to FAME, and wound up writing for their publishing staff there for a while.

Jason Isbell played this 1956 Martin D-18 on his albums *Something More Than Free* and *The Nashville Sound.*

ARTIFACT COURTESY OF JASON ISBELL

OPPOSITE PAGE: Handwritten lyrics by Jason Isbell to "24 Frames," named the Best American Roots Song at the *58th Annual Grammy Awards* in 2016.

ARTIFACT COURTESY OF JASON ISBELL

I was really self-conscious, because I thought, "Well, this is not going to be a country hit. This song doesn't have a chorus." But Rodney Hall would hear the songs, and he just would be blown away. Sometimes he would say, "Maybe let me try one that's a little more middle of the road." But most of the time, he was just giving me really positive feedback on types of songs that he hadn't necessarily heard before. It occurred to me: "If I just keep writing really good songs, I don't have to try to shape them into any particular genre or into any particular box."

You could expand that to represent the whole spirit of the place. That's probably the point of everything that I know about the Shoals. If the songs are good enough, and the stories you're telling are good enough, then everything else will figure itself out. That's a lot of what this book is about, too: how Muscle Shoals figured out what it could be, how a small town made a big sound heard round the world. You'll learn more about that in this catalog, which is the companion to *Low Rhythm Rising*, the major exhibition launched in the fall of 2025 by the Country Music Hall of Fame and Museum.

I hope the book and the exhibit take you right back into the mighty music of Muscle Shoals, a place where everyday people found a way to build something extraordinary and enduring just dreaming and working together.

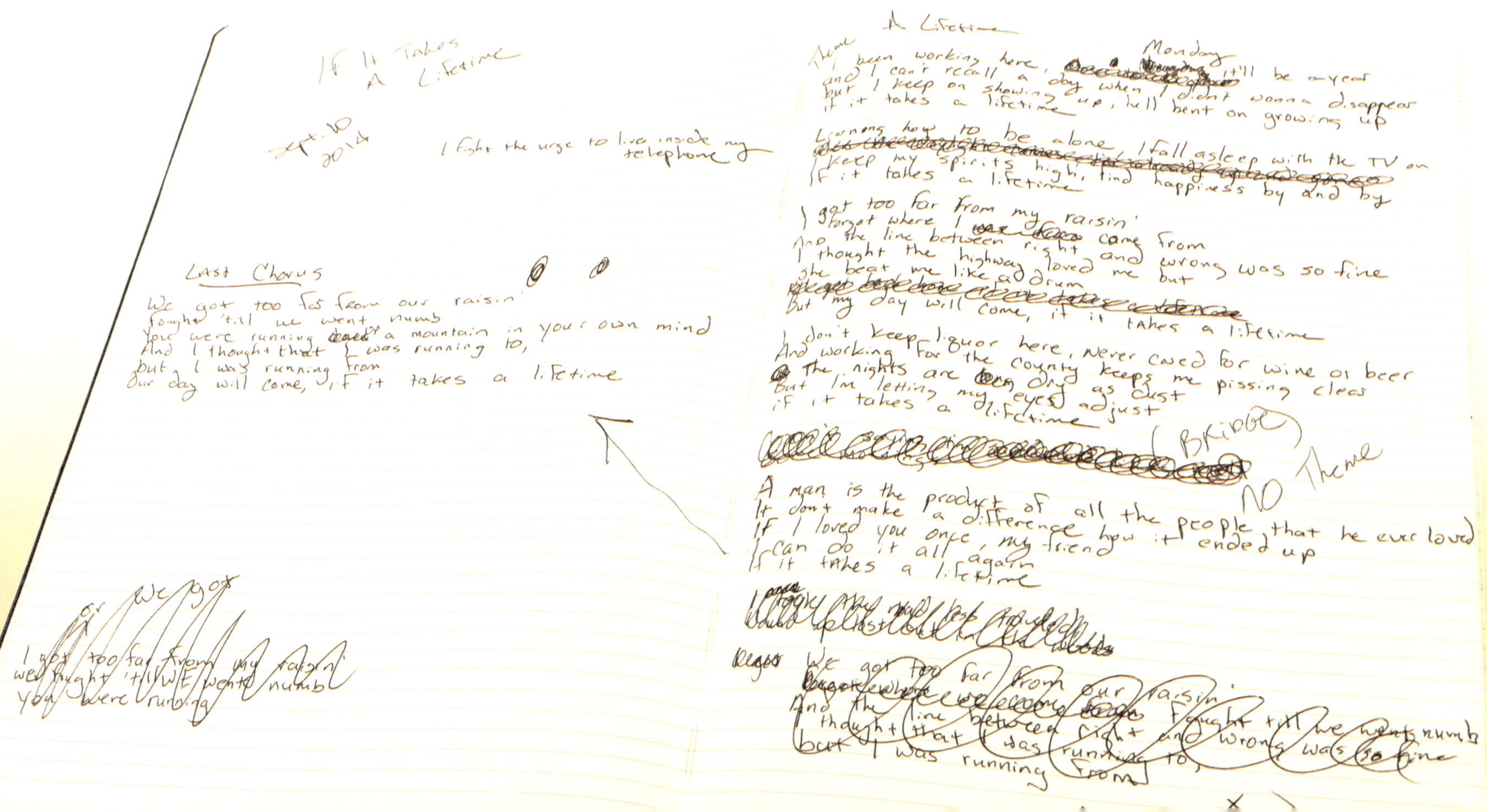

A view of Wilson Reservoir at Muscle Shoals, formed by Wilson Dam.
The dam was named after President Woodrow Wilson. It was completed in 1925.

PHOTO COURTESY OF THE ALABAMA DEPARTMENT OF HISTORY

ANYTHING THAT YOU AIN'T SUPPOSED TO DO, BUT YOU CAN GET AWAY WITH

BY RJ SMITH

By the time John Donelson, frontiersman, speculator, and founder of Nashville, arrived at the place on the Tennessee River that is the subject of this book and exhibition, many bad things had happened. It was 1779 and his party had ventured west to Alabama, along the Cumberland and Ohio rivers to the Tennessee looking for land to settle. His party had been attacked by Native Americans and suffered smallpox, extreme cold, and hunger. Their flatboats and canoes had made it this far, to a danger zone earlier visitors had dubbed "The Whirl," or "The Suck."

When Donelson's boats arrived there, the water suddenly fell out beneath them as they descended through fast currents, then exploded on the rocks at the bottom of the drop, where the river seemed to flow in all directions at once. Here was the spot he had heard of, a place where a community might be established. A future, if the present allowed for one. At the moment, though, Donelson just wondered how soon the boats would all be destroyed "and all our troubles ended at once."

He remembered the sound of the place, writing in his journal, "The water being high made a terrible roaring, which could be heard at some distance." It was called Muscle Shoals. Smashed bits of boats rested on shallow rocks.

Some 180 years later, new driftwood gathered in Muscle Shoals, Alabama. As usual, the ne'er-do-wells met in the funky rooms above a pharmacy in Florence, Alabama, not far from the river. They were musicians and songwriters. Hungry fiddlers and rockabilly fans and uncategorizable others. At the crux was the man who lived there, the manager of a local movie theater named Tom Stafford. The charismatic Stafford had scoliosis, which curved his spine so much it made him look, he liked to say,

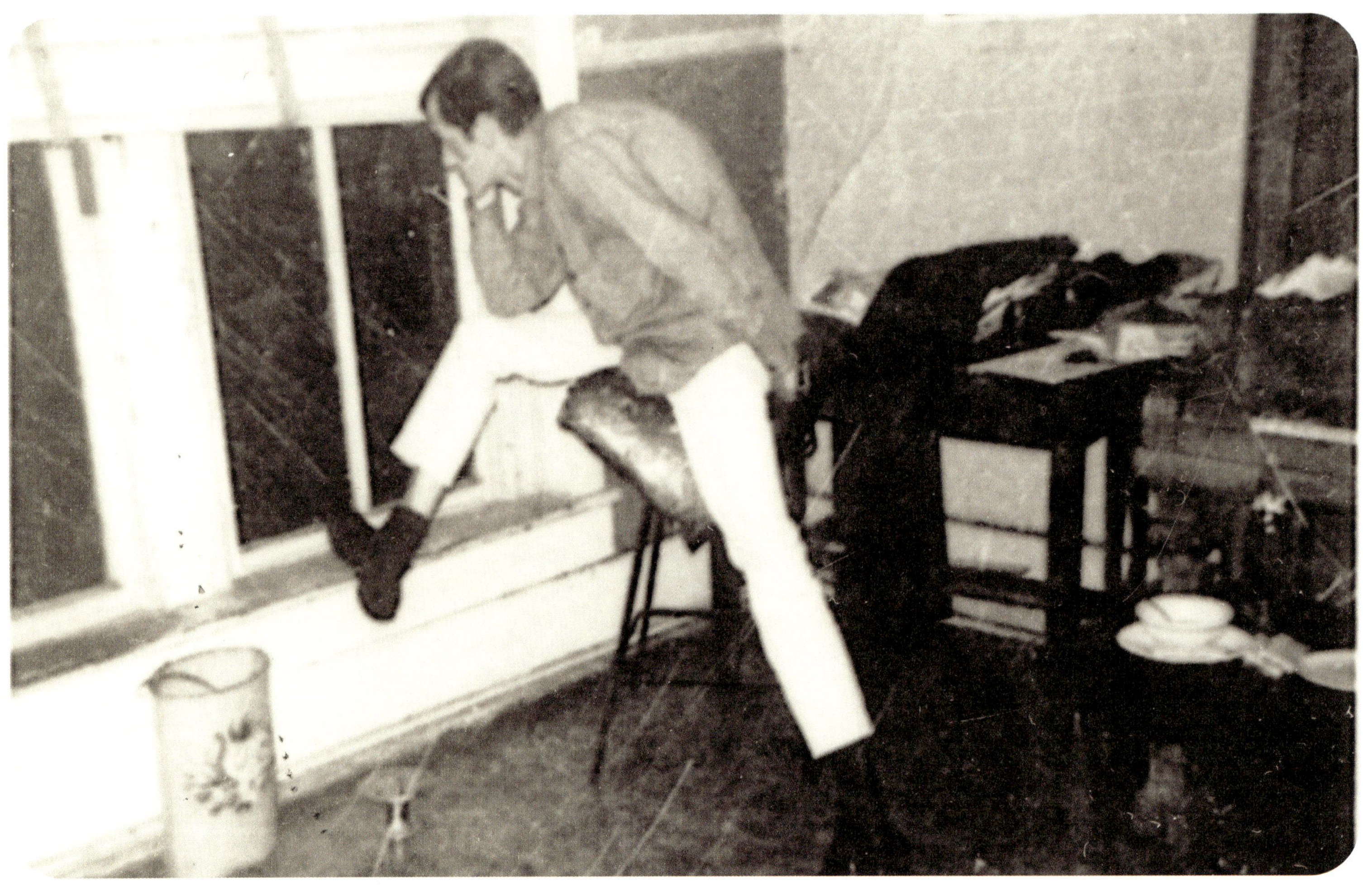

Tom Stafford looks out over Tennessee Street from his rented space above City Drug Store, Florence, Alabama, c. 1960. PHOTO COURTESY OF RICHARD YOUNGER

like a walking question mark. In his space, they passed medicines and guitars around, and the question mark drove it into the ragged bunch that music wasn't something that happened to you, it was something that you made. You can write good songs, he repeated a hundred different ways. You could record them. You could make your own hit records.

Stafford seemed to know things and shared his knowledge with a fervor that would have done John Donelson proud. He had rented a couple of rooms that were formerly a podiatrist's office. This place on top of the City Drug Store was a whirl, too, and a profound time suck, pulling newcomers in to scream and shout and argue about the world. They would write some good songs.

Stafford had gotten $300 from a fledgling record man who managed the Florence bus depot, and he began turning his place into a recording studio. He hung a sign: "Spar Music // commercial recordings // songs published."

The front entrance of Spar Music in downtown Florence, Alabama, c. 1959. Tom Stafford opened the studio with a $300 investment from Tune Records founder James Joiner.

PHOTO COURTESY OF FAME RECORDING STUDIOS

Songwriter and musician Dan Penn in front of the hearse used by his band Dan Penn & the Pallbearers in the early 1960s. The group often played the fraternity circuit when Penn worked as FAME Studio's first resident songwriter. PHOTO COURTESY OF DAN PENN

One of the regulars was a young songwriter from Vernon, Alabama, named Dan Penn. He settled in fast after his first visit. "I walked in the studio and there were four cots on the floor," he said, each of them occupied by local musicians. "This was the middle of the day and these guys were sleeping as late as they wanted. I thought, This is it!"

He set a strong tone from the moment you met him, recalled the late songwriter John D. Wyker. Penn was probably sixteen when Wyker saw him at Spar. Wyker wrote about the encounter years later in rapid-fire style. "He was dressed in a brown leather jacket . . . he had a white T-shirt on and blue denim jeans, probably Levis . . . and a pair of brown leather house shoes. . . .

"Dan was also wearing a hat . . . it was what we called a black stingy brim hat . . . much like the Blues Brothers would make famous many years later. . . . Penn wore sunglasses at night." Wyker was amazed. "Penn's right hand was all bandaged up . . . gauze covered two or three fingers and wrapped up around his wrist . . . he was walkin' down the hall of Spar . . . which was a real small place, and somebody I think it was Norbert or Briggs or Carrigan yelled at Dan and asked him, 'What happened to your hand Dan?'. . . . Penn replied 'KNIFE FIGHT!' . . . and never missed a beat as he spit his gum like a bullet from the barrel of a pistol into a waiting metal garbage can . . . PING!"

Stafford waved an envelope at Penn; it would be his first check, for his song "Is a Blue Bird Blue," a Conway Twitty hit in 1960. "Dan never broke stride as he fired back, 'Good, I need to buy me a new car 'cause that old used car I'm drivin' just blew an engine!' Tom asked him how that happened, and Dan fired back, 'Draggin' for pink slips!'"

Dan Penn wore this floral brocade jacket in the early 1960s, as the lead singer with the Mark V, an R&B band from Florence, Alabama.

ARTIFACT COURTESY OF DAN PENN

Dates and details vary, but it is agreed that a community unlike anything found in the rest of the Shoals was taking shape at Spar. Most everyone of the guys up in Stafford's place was white, but around the time Penn arrived a steady-natured, tall Black

Arthur Alexander's passport, 1966

ARTIFACT COURTESY OF RICHARD YOUNGER

OPPOSITE PAGE: **Arthur Alexander in performance, 1963. By this time, Alexander had a pop hit with "You Better Move On."**

PHOTO COURTESY OF RICHARD YOUNGER

songwriter and singer named Arthur Alexander also became a regular. Everybody called him June, for Junior, because his dad was Arthur Sr. He had grown up in East Florence, attending a segregated school but playing mostly with white kids in the neighborhood. The Shoals was like that—public spaces were policed, but the rules were blurred in more private areas. June loved Black vocal groups as well as singing cowboys like Roy Rogers and Gene Autry. He cited Hank Williams as a key influence on his style. In sixth grade, he formed a doo-wop group named the Heartstrings that appeared on a local TV station's Saturday morning teen music show.

Alexander was interested in making his own records, and as a teenager he made a point of connecting with acts like the Clovers and Clyde McPhatter when they came through town, asking them how they wrote songs, and what choices led to a hit.

By the late 1950s, young white rock & roll bands were forming around all four cities that together formed greater Muscle Shoals—Florence, Sheffield, Muscle Shoals, and Tuscumbia. Their members came to the rooms above City Drug Store, and besides Alexander their names included Penn, Spooner Oldham, Rick Hall, David Hood, Jerry Carrigan, Roger Hawkins, Norbert Putnam, David Briggs, Marlin Greene, Earl "Peanutt" Montgomery, Donnie Fritts, and many others.

June Alexander, sometimes with Black friends, was coming by Stafford's place for the same reason the white rock & rollers were: to share their passions and find out how to make a life out of them. He kept coming, and the others enjoyed the company of the slim, tall songwriter who held a lot of country in his voice.

They were working on the same basic project, nothing on the line, nothing but the hopes and dreams of everybody in the room. They played their songs to one another. "We would sit down, you know, and no matter what song it was—if it was a rhythm & blues song or a country song—we approached it with the same vigor," Alexander recalled. "We didn't make choices, I guess, until later, when people started putting labels on stuff. That was way down the line."

The Del-Rays perform at a sorority dance, early 1960s. Jimmy Johnson (guitar) became part of the Muscle Shoals Rhythm Section at FAME Studio, then founded Muscle Shoals Sound Studio with fellow Swampers David Hood, Barry Beckett, and Roger Hawkins.

FROM LEFT: Jimmy Ray Hunter, Larry York, Jimmy Johnson, Bill Scott, and Bill Cofield

PHOTO COURTESY OF MARK BECKETT

E ROSE BALL
ΚΔ

Wilson Dam—Rough Water Muscle Shoals Florence, Ala.

Wilson Dam on the Tennessee River connects the towns of Florence and Muscle Shoals.

PHOTO COURTESY OF THE LIBRARY OF CONGRESS

ALTERNATING CURRENTS

This intersection—of races, sounds, attitudes—was the beginning of the Muscle Shoals music scene. A lot flowed out of the place in the years ahead. But it's worth pulling back and looking at forces that shaped the region in the time just before.

By the early decades of the twentieth century, the river Donelson came down continued to attract folks who saw greater possibilities if only the Tennessee's currents could be tamed. During World War I, a national effort to dam the river and harness its hydroelectric potential was launched. Thousands of workers flocked to the region's government-built villages—a white one and a Black one. Leaders saw an opportunity to help America in World War I and develop the region once the war ended.

Thomas Edison and Henry Ford leaned in, the latter advancing flamboyant plans for a visionary "seventy-five-mile-long city" that would produce cars with new technology while electricity from the dam would transform the lives of Alabama farmers. Some 18,000 workers came to the Shoals to build the Wilson Dam, and by the time it was finished in 1925, the modern Muscle Shoals was emerging.

The vast possibilities had also brought a flood of developers, and real estate boomed. Sidewalks were hastily built across cotton fields, streets were gridded for acres in anticipation of the coming Ford City. But as the Depression deepened, elected officials

began to argue that the American public, rather than any private sector tech bro, should be in control of something this transformative. By the early 1930s, President Roosevelt had viewed the Wilson Dam and called for its use as part of the New Deal that was rebuilding America. The Wilson Dam became a central feature of the brand-new Tennessee Valley Authority, an entity that has taken many forms over its nine decades but that was created as a public institution to develop energy, infrastructure, small farms, and rural communities.

The river is one through line leading to Muscle Shoals. Another is the presence of Black life. In that realm, Willie Ruff was a through line all unto himself. Born in 1931, right as Congress was debating whether to make the Wilson Dam public property, Ruff was a Black kid growing up in Sheffield. Across the street was a white pal who taught him how to play the drums on his front lawn. Ruff had a lifelong love of music; he grew up to be a fine jazz musician and professor of music at Yale for nearly fifty years.

As a writer and talker, Ruff shed a lot of light on music created in the Shoals. He sang for change in Sheffield candy stores as a kid. "St. Louis Blues" was a tune he knew by heart. That number was one of the many written by W. C. Handy, who was born in Florence in 1873, to parents who had been enslaved.

TOP: W. C. Handy, born in Florence, Alabama, was one of the first musicians to formalize, publish, and popularize the blues for a mass audience.

BOTTOM: Published in 1914, W. C. Handy's "St. Louis Blues" is now considered one of the most influential songs in American history.

This barn dance took place during the construction of Wheeler Dam in Sheffield, Alabama, 1932. PHOTO COURTESY OF FLORENCE-LAUDERDALE PUBLIC LIBRARY

Handy composed and published many early blues numbers, but "St Louis Blues" is his most famous. His childhood cabin today is the W. C. Handy Museum. While Ruff was in grade school, Handy came back home, a mogul whose words held special sway in his hometown. He visited Ruff's Baptist schoolhouse and played "Go Down Moses" on his trumpet. When the visit was over, Handy shook hands with the students. Ruff went home glowing.

"I said, 'Damn, that hand has done something today,'" Ruff said in a 2023 interview. "That hand had shook the hand that wrote 'St. Louis Blues.'" He told his mother he planned to never wash it again. "She said, 'You gonna wash it again before you come to my dinner table.' . . . So I said 'Well, I think I can sop as good with the left as I can with this one, so if I keep this one behind my back can I eat with this one?'" It was the day "Mr. Handy became my man."

Ruff connected later generations to the great music that came out of Muscle Shoals. He recalled the swinging calliope men who played the flatboats on the river. He and his neighbor would wait, almost in view of Handy's birthplace, and listen for the boats going by. In his autobiography, Ruff described how the community came out to listen: "Icemen, shoeshine boys, maids, and hoboes, all friends of mine, lined the levee to listen to the jazzman 'play that thing till it rained on him.' The 'rain' was just condensed steam from the calliope, falling back to soak the player's straw hat, his red-and-white-striped shirt with fancy sleeve garters. . . . "

Ruff was friends with record producer John Hammond, and one day the two got to talking about the Shoals region. A lover of

Growing up in Alabama, drummer Roger Hawkins became immersed in early R&B and country music he heard on this Zenith console tube radio.

ARTIFACT COURTESY OF BILLY LAWSON

OPPOSITE PAGE: Sheffield native Willie Ruff playing bass at a club he owned in New Haven, Connecticut, c. 1960. He taught at Yale School of Music for forty-six years.

blues and jazz, Hammond had covered the trial of the Scottsboro Boys in Decatur, Alabama, in 1931 for the *Nation* magazine. During a break, he stood outside the courthouse and asked a local, "Do I have to go all the way to Birmingham to hear some good Black music?"

No, he was told. "You can get plenty of that in Sheffield."

There was great music being made in Sheffield and the rest of the Shoals long before studios were able to record it. The music reached across all sorts of lines. But there were boundaries nonetheless, and crossing them remained perilous. Race relations might not have been as violent as they were in bigger Alabama cities to the south like Birmingham and Montgomery. Historians have offered several possible reasons that the Shoals never became a cauldron.

One idea is that cotton plantations this far north of the Mississippi Delta were often smaller and treated the enslaved less brutally, setting a regional tone. It has also been suggested that businessmen and government officials flocking to the Shoals after World War I, offering jobs and government contracts, encouraged a degree of community harmony as a condition of federal support.

"It is clear in the historical record that the Shoals had relatively few incidents of racial unrest and white supremacist violence compared with the rest of the state and that integration seems to have come somewhat voluntarily and mostly peacefully," according to the website of the Civil Rights Struggle in the Shoals Project 1945–1975. "At the same time, it seems clear that the size of the Black population in the four cities had something important to do with the nature of race relations."

The Quad Cities region is spread across two counties, Colbert and Lauderdale. Scholar Christopher M. Riali, sifting 1940 census data, notes that Alabama as a whole was 75 percent white and 25 percent Black, but in Colbert and Lauderdale counties it was 80 percent white and 20 percent Black. Meanwhile the Black population was far larger in cities like Birmingham and Montgomery.

These demographics themselves frustrated efforts to create equality. Huston Cobb Jr. worked for the TVA after World War II and was a civil rights figure in the Shoals. In an oral history, he described why there was no social movement comparable to, say, the Birmingham bus boycott in the 1950s. "You didn't need no movement," he explained. "You wasn't going to get . . . nowhere. There wasn't enough of you."

With fewer potential boycotters, the economic impact would have been severely limited. And with so few Black voters on hand, there was less in the way of poll taxes and voter intimidation: "You couldn't vote nobody out," as one Black resident expressed it.

Josephine Ford was a Black woman and a recruiter for the TVA. To an interviewer she described the bus boycotts and sit-ins going on in Alabama in the 1950s and 1960s: "We knew that bad things were happening in those other areas," said Ford.

Postcard depicting an aerial view of Sheffield, Alabama. PHOTO COURTESY OF UNIVERSITY OF NORTH ALABAMA ARCHIVES AND SPECIAL COLLECTIONS

Police carrying away George Edward Davis for participating in a Montgomery, Alabama, sit-in, 1965. PHOTO COURTESY OF THE ALABAMA DEPARTMENT OF HISTORY

"But here it was kind of quiet, under the surface. It wasn't like it was in those other areas." There was not a critical mass that could make demands on a white majority, she noted. "[But] we were just as upset, and we kept up with what was going on, trust me."

"Really, you were supposed to get off the sidewalk if a white was coming; you were supposed to step off. And that was just the law. That's it, you know. Unless you wanted to go to jail," recalled David M. Smith.

The dynamics of working in a small-town, quasi-rural area of the South presented special barriers to activism. "One reason why is that we all worked for the people you [would be] protesting against, so you'd get fired," explained Smith. A lack of the kind of violent incidents that made history in other areas does not tell anything like the whole story of relations in the Shoals. Newspaper accounts from the years after the Civil War suggest it was a place where interracial confrontations on the street repeatedly ended with Black men being shot. More often, this was a place where the fear of violence was enough to dominate an outnumbered Black population. Let's put it this way: In 1960, three dozen Black college students staged a sit-in at the segregated lunch counter of the Montgomery County Courthouse. When the governor expelled them from Alabama State University, over a thousand marched to the state capitol in support.

A year later, a man named Charlie Brown went to the lunch counter of the Spalding Drug store in downtown Florence and ordered lunch. After a long practice of being fed in the kitchen,

The Tri-C

Dedicated To The Interest Of The P

E A Service SHEFFIELD, TUSCUMBIA, MUSCLE SHOALS CITY

Possible Local 'Sit-In' Attempt Reported Today

What could possibly be the beginning of a "sit-in" attempt at local eating establishments was reported shortly after noon today by the police department.

A Negro named Charlie Brown, employed by a downtown store, reportedly entered Spalding Drug Co., corner Court and Mobile Sts., shortly before noon and took a seat at a lunch counter.

Store officials, who said that the Negro had been fed in the kitchen for a long time, said he was asked to leave by employes and that when he made no effort to do so, the police were called, and Brown was taken into custody and placed in the city jail, pending charges.

Chief of Police Noah H. Danley said the Negro was taken into custody by Captain Robert Anderson and Policeman Voyd Lambert.

The police chief said he did not know what action would be taken and at press time was trying to reach Mayor E. F. Martin, who was inspecting a construction project when the case developed, and City Attorney Arnold Teks.

Police said they did not know what charge would be preferred against the Negro, but presumed he would be charged with breach of the peace.

Police said they did not know the Negro's age or his home address and were continuing their investigation.

Over 100 Kil

Murder

Afterm

HURRICANE'S LITTER

...ir of gannets ...y're seen on

Headline from Sheffield's *Tri-Cities Daily* newspaper, November 2, 1961

Brown wanted to be served the way white patrons were. "Possible Local 'Sit-In' Attempt Reported Today," a frontpage story of a Shoals newspaper reported on November 2, 1961. He was one guy, by himself, insisting he be served. In Florence, Alabama, they arrested Charlie Brown and jailed him overnight without charges.

WHO'S KNOCKIN'?

Meanwhile, folks kept coming by Tom Stafford's place. They were drawn by the lack of boredom, by Stafford's ability to talk about comic books and movies and poetry and life in the Shoals, his ability with his curved spine to fold up like a meditating bat while he considered what you said and then to fill the void with his expansive response. They were there for his rapid-fire homily: that making records in the Shoals was possible and necessary. Right now.

For the most part, the musicians coming to Spar Music were running from their past. They had grown up, most of them, hearing music at square dances, fiddle contests, shape-note gospel gatherings, and on the radio broadcasts of the Grand Ole Opry. They had been raised to love country music, and suddenly their love went sideways, now that rock & roll was playing. Some remembered hearing Florence-born Sam Phillips in the early 1940s, broadcasting country and gospel on local radio station WLAY. More of them were now hearing the blues and rock & roll Phillips was recording in Memphis that was played on WLAY's race-mixing "open playlist" format.

The Fairlanes, late 1950s, a key incubator for Shoals talent.
FROM LEFT TO RIGHT: Rick Hall, Charlie Senn, Randy Allen, Billy Sherrill, and Terry Thompson
PHOTO COURTESY OF FAME RECORDING STUDIOS

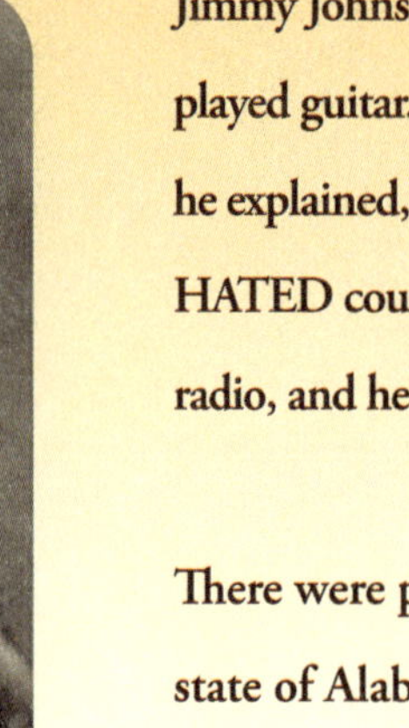

Jimmy Johnson grew up in a Sheffield house where both parents played guitar. They wanted him to learn. "But they couldn't get me," he explained, "because they both played country music and I HATED country music." He had just discovered Chuck Berry on the radio, and he knew immediately: "I have to learn how to play that."

There were probably no proper recording studios in the entire state of Alabama in the 1950s. For that matter, there were more—a lot more—*milkshake cups* scattered across Tom Stafford's piano than there were *im*proper studios in the state of Alabama in the decade. But change was afoot.

Dexter Johnson was a turbine operator for the TVA who had played guitar and mandolin in bluegrass group the Blue Seal Pals. The Pals had a radio show in the Shoals in the early 1940s. A decade later Dexter, who was Jimmy Johnson's uncle, built a demo studio in his Sheffield garage, the first commercial studio in the region. Inspired by Johnson, James Joiner co-founded Tune Records in 1956. His family ran the Joiner Bus company, which picked up rural folks from points distant and brought

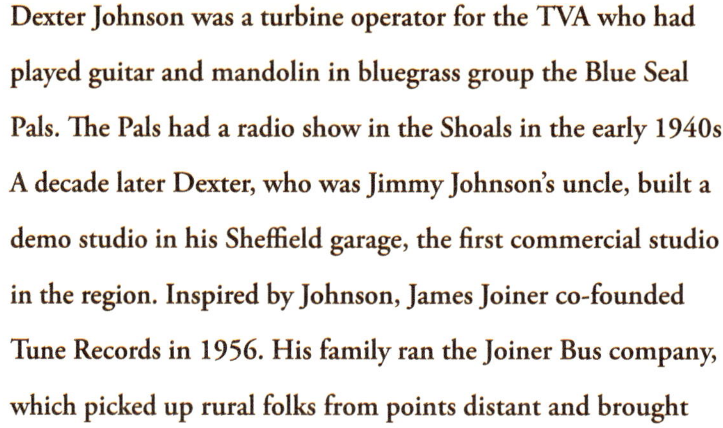

TOP: Junior Thompson from Florence recorded the classic singles "Who's Knocking?" and "Raw Deal" in 1956.

BOTTOM: Sun Records founder and Country Music Hall of Fame member Sam Phillips wore this Coffee High School jacket when he was in marching band in Florence, Alabama, c. 1940.

ARTIFACT COURTESY OF JERRY PHILLIPS

OPPOSITE PAGE: James Joiner used this Concertone reel-to-reel tape recorder at early Tune recording sessions, in the late 1950s.

ARTIFACT COURTESY OF THE ALABAMA MUSIC HALL OF FAME

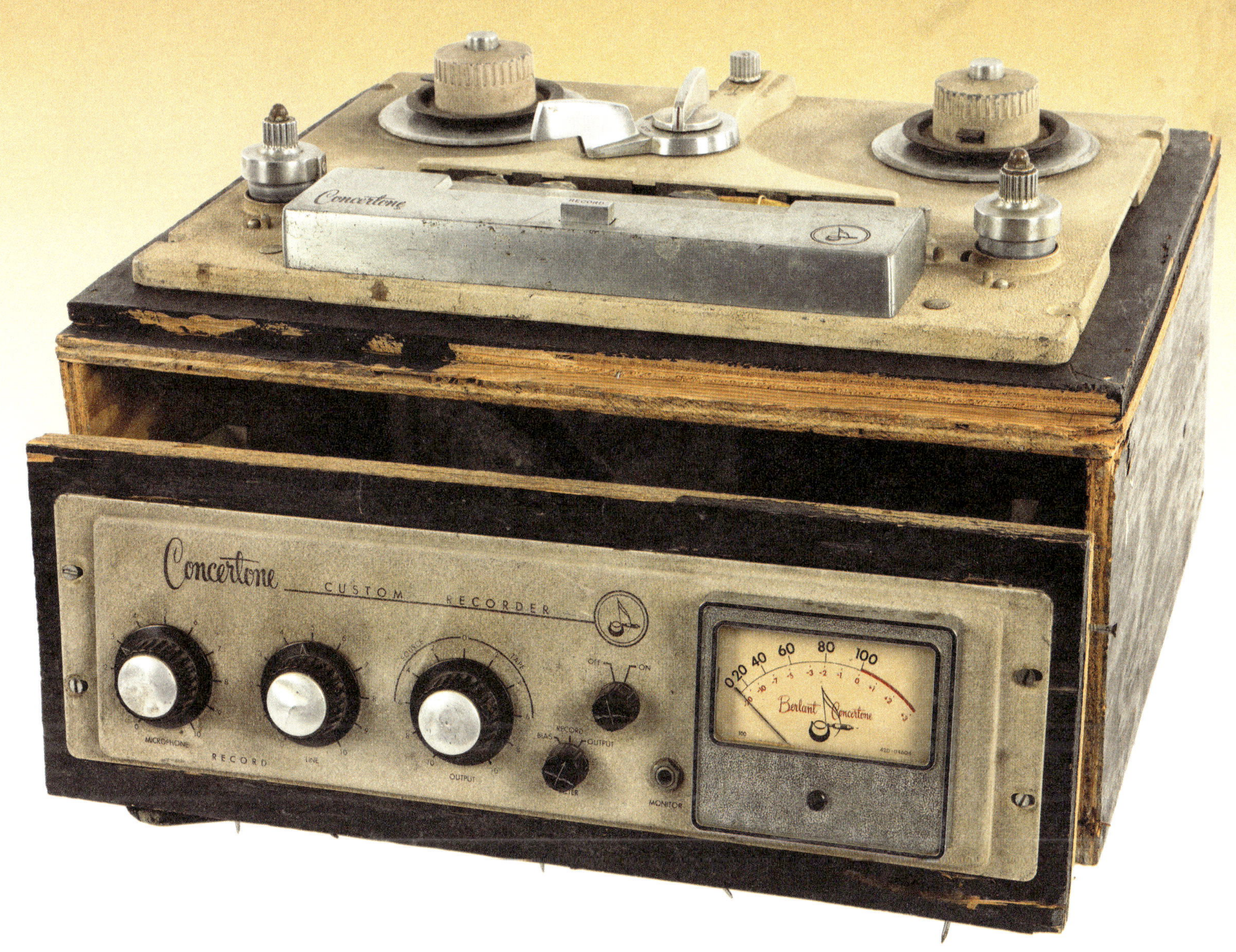

them into the Shoals. On Sundays, Joiner would push tables and chairs around the Florence bus station restaurant and set up a two-track recorder and microphones. Tune produced Junior Thompson's amazing rockabilly hallucination "Who's Knocking?" in 1956. This was the first record released on Alabama's first label. A year later, Tune had a local hit with the teen country ballad "A Fallen Star," by future Alabama governor Bobby Denton. Flushed with success, Joiner passed $300 to help Tom Stafford set up Spar.

When June Alexander arrived, things were shaken up further. And then a driven, exasperating agent of change named Rick Hall immediately went after the future with a perilous certainty that left everybody else far behind him in the red Alabama clay. Once he had made it in the world, Hall played the role of rustic sage for eager reporters. Of growing up in Freedom Hills, Alabama, he said, "Shoot, man, if I was to have painted myself green and stood beside a three-year-old pine sapling, you couldn't have told us apart, I was so stark skinny."

Drafted into the U.S. Army during the Korean War in the early 1950s, Rick Hall declared himself a conscientious objector. While in the service, he played in a band for the honor guard of the Fourth United States Army. PHOTO COURTESY OF MUSCLE SHOALS SOUND STUDIOS

But Hall's was a terrible existence—his mom had left his impoverished family for a more sustainable life of prostitution, and his dad raised Rick and his sister in a dirt-floor sawmiller shack. "We learned to live like animals in order to survive," he said.

Following a stint in the army after the Korean War, Hall played in country bands and worked in the Reynolds Metals plant in Sheffield. Hall made trips to Nashville trying to sell country songs he had written. By the mid-1950s, he had joined a

RIGHT: This fiddle belonged to Rick Hall. As a teenager, he played at country square dances with his group the Country Pals.

ARTIFACT COURTESY OF FAME RECORDING STUDIOS

BELOW: Promotional poster for the Fairlanes, which included Rick Hall, Terry Thompson, Billy Sherrill, Charlie Senn, and Randy Allen, late 1950s.

ARTIFACT COURTESY OF FAME RECORDING STUDIOS

Arthur Alexander recorded his debut single, "Sally Sue Brown," for Judd, the label owned by Jud Phillips, the brother of Sun Records founder Sam Phillips. Released in 1960, the song was covered by Bob Dylan on his 1988 album, *Down in the Groove.*

ARTIFACT COURTESY OF RICHARD YOUNGER

OPPOSITE PAGE: Arthur Alexander performing at the Flamingo Club during a three-week tour of England, 1966. Alexander referred to the tour as "the highlight of my life."

PHOTO BY BILL MILLAR. COURTESY OF RICHARD YOUNGER

fledgling rock & roll band, the Fairlanes, with a local buddy, Billy Sherrill. Both were proudly arrogant, certain they were smarter than their peers and better than the guys they were playing music with. Nobody had nothing, yet, and the two acted out their self-confidence whenever they dropped by Tom Stafford's studio.

All of these pups were voracious converts to R&B and rock & roll. Like Elvis from Memphis, they were part of a Southern generation imbibing the new stuff, white kids trying to sound like their new Black heroes. They formed bands like the Pallbearers and the Mark V and played parties and frat houses and raced out to the state line bars a short drive north, where the dry laws did not apply, learning how to rock tough crowds. They played forbidden music—Black music—in the Jim Crow South.

And unlike Elvis, they had a Black hero in the room with them: June Alexander. They couldn't sit with him at a local show, but they sat on a bench and wrote songs together for hours in the space above City Drug Store.

Alexander's first breakthrough, "Sally Sue Brown," was a blues about a bad girl coming back to town. It said *watch out* and *can't wait* at the same time. Alexander brought the song in his head to Spar, revised it with Tom Stafford and Earl "Peanutt" Montgomery, and recorded it. It was released on the Judd label in 1960; few heard it at the time, but among those who have heard it since are Bob Dylan and Elvis Costello, both of whom have covered the song.

Arthur Alexander recording at Bradley Studios in Nashville, 1963. PHOTO BY JIMMY ELLIS / *THE TENNESSEAN*

This is the copy of Arthur Alexander's "You Better Move On" that Rick Hall gave to his mother, Dollie. ARTIFACT COURTESY OF FAME RECORDING STUDIOS

"Sally Sue Brown" sounds raw and fully formed; it has echo and mud on it, and both are as essential as any instrument present—other than Alexander's piercing voice.

The debut showed the gathered that they were getting somewhere. Hall and Sherrill threw in with Stafford to form a publishing company called FAME—Florence Alabama Music Enterprises—and signed Alexander. It was an important start, even if it turned out to be a false one: Sherrill quit while watching *North by Northwest* at the movies, when Hall busted in to berate him for not working hard enough. Hall kept the name and doubled down on his plans; Sherrill headed to Nashville.

Scotch

Resentment would become Hall's spiritual nourishment. He was quick to feel aggrieved, abandoned. What followed would be a recurring pattern in his brilliant life—acute acrimony, used to fuel amazing work. He would show them.

Hall found a former tobacco and candy warehouse out by Wilson Dam and fixed it up as a studio. He and his fellow Fairlane Terry Thompson became FAME songwriters, and played on demos recorded at the warehouse studio while they continued teaching each other how to make a record.

Then came an unexpected windfall. Stafford had a new killer song that Alexander had written, and he needed a studio better than his to record it. "Tom Stafford had to eat crow and call me for help with Arthur Alexander," Hall remembered a bit gleefully later on. With a great talent humbly heading his way, things were looking up.

In his fine biography of Alexander, author Richard Younger describes him standing in the lobby of the Muscle Shoals Hotel, dressed in his brown bellhop uniform with beige piping and a tight little cap, humming to himself. It was a song gently, firmly steering a suitor away from the woman he loves. Alexander was thinking about the hits on the radio, full-voiced R&B songs made by Ben E. King and the Drifters, and tailored his tune to their dimensions as he moved through the hotel halls.

With easygoing charm, the song, "You Better Move On," splits the difference between country and rhythm & blues; even as it

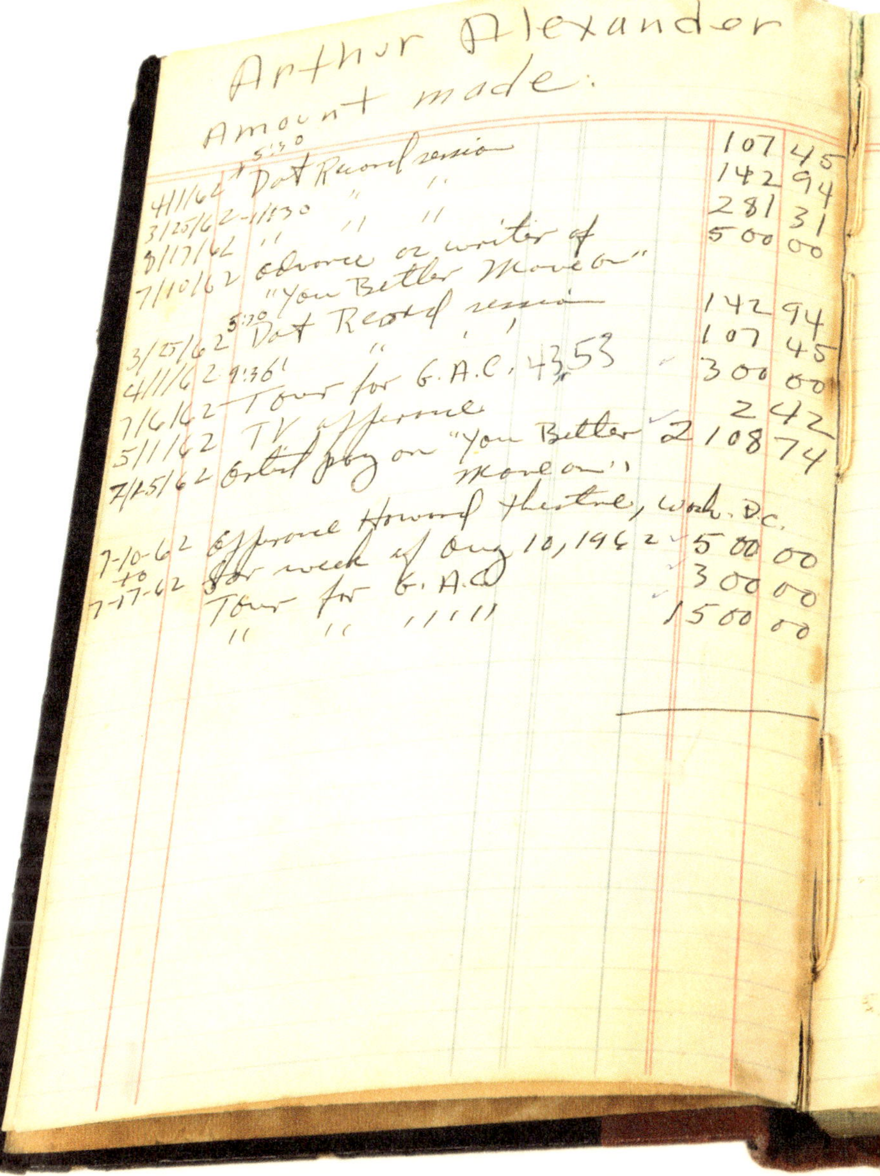

Arthur Alexander used this ledger to document payments received from Dot Records recording sessions, tours, and TV appearances in 1962.

ARTIFACT COURTESY OF RICHARD YOUNGER

OPPOSITE PAGE: Rick Hall behind the sound board at the original location of FAME, early 1960s.

PHOTO COURTESY OF FAME RECORDING STUDIOS

ends with a warning ("I'm getting mighty mad") it lands as a confession, truth telling, an unburdening somewhere between the barstool and the church pew.

Stafford was all-in to get it made, hocking his own recording equipment to pay for the session at Hall's studio. Hall hired a handful of the Spar crew to back Alexander. Adopting what he called a "kill attitude," he recorded the song over and over for days. Hall took the tape to Nashville, where they repeatedly failed to get a deal until WMAK rock & roll DJ Noel Ball heard it and reached out to LA-based Dot Records, formerly a Nashville-area label that had launched Pat Boone as a national popstar. The Alexander single that Dot released, with the sweetly stomping "A Shot of Rhythm & Blues" on the B-side, came out in December 1961. It slowly worked its way up the charts, reaching #24 by February 1962.

His records that immediately followed—"Soldier of Love (Lay Down Your Arms)," "Anna," and "Go Home Girl," all from 1962—share an easygoing generosity. His vocals make

an open-faced appeal, baring difficult feelings in a matter-of-fact way. Artlessness hangs over them, and he embodies a simple guy standing alone, making a public appeal of his complicated feelings. This was Charlie Brown addressing the crowd, one guy finding the boldness that he would never fully push back down ever again. "You Better Move On" was the beginning of the Muscle Shoals sound, a hitmaking approach featuring a Black singer, white musicians backing with an encompassing clarity that pinpointed a zone where country and soul fused. Alexander himself would not record in the Shoals again until 1968, but his impact hung over a growing recording enterprise that gained national attention over the next few years.

OPPOSITE PAGE: After Rick Hall took ownership of FAME in 1960, he set up a studio in this warehouse on Wilson Dam Highway in Muscle Shoals.

PHOTO COURTESY OF KEVIN LAMB

ABOVE: With the success of Arthur Alexander's "You Better Move On," Rick Hall was able to move FAME Studio to this building at 603 East Avalon Avenue in Muscle Shoals. The studio is still in operation at that location.

PHOTO BY JIMMY JOHNSON. COURTESY OF FAME RECORDING STUDIOS

REDWAL MU

SOUL MUSIC

If you head southeast from the Wilson Dam and zig zag about fifteen miles, you'll come upon the small town of Leighton. Around the time that Alexander was hitting the road in the early 1960s to make the most of his moment, a diminutive fellow from Leighton caught Alexander in action, and that moment changed the next few years of his life.

Jimmy Hughes had his feet firmly planted in what's possible. He knew Alexander from the local night clubs, but hearing "You Better Move On" didn't turn his head. Hughes was getting all the attention he needed performing in Leighton's gospel quartet the Singing Clouds, when he wasn't working nights at the ES Robbins Floor Products plant in Tuscumbia. Then one day Hughes spotted Alexander behind the wheel of a brand-new Lincoln automobile, and that was it. "I said, 'I'm going to get me one of those,'" Hughes told me. "It changed my mind."

He went to Black entrepreneur Bob Carl Bailey, who owned a pool hall in Leighton and worked for the car dealership where Hall was also employed. Introduction made. That led to a FAME recording session, which was remarkable in several ways. First because it was brilliant—"Steal Away" is a gorgeous plea to a lady to drop whatever she was doing late one night and pay Jimmy a call.

Phil and Alan Walden (left) greet Percy Sledge, Jimmy Hughes, and Quin Ivy in Macon, Georgia, c. 1966. Phil Walden developed meaningful ties to Muscle Shoals on his way to opening Capricorn Records in 1969. MICHAEL OCHS ARCHIVE/GETTY IMAGES

LEFT: In 1963 Jimmy Hughes reworked the old gospel standard "Steal Away" into a secular hit.

RIGHT: *Billboard* advertisement, 1964.

COURTESY OF FAME RECORDING STUDIOS

"I was just writing a story and sang it down," said Hughes. "If you listen to it real good, it sort of has a gospel thing because that's the way I sang all my life. And it sounded like a gospel song, the way I sang." It sure does—"Steal Away to Jesus" was a nineteenth-century spiritual touchstone, still sung in churches when Hughes was coming up.

This was soul music. Dan Penn happened to be around when Hughes recorded, and he held "Steal Away" in high regard. After it sat on FAME shelves for almost two years, one day Penn asked Hall what happened to that good tune. They gave it another listen, and the two pledged to try once more. Hughes re-recorded it, and Penn and Hall drove around the South, visiting Black DJs with a car full of records and a case of vodka, until they finally broke "Steal Away." It went to #17 on *Billboard*'s Hot 100 during the summer of 1964 and, more to the point, deserves credit as being "a song so good, it would basically create the whole concept of Southern Soul," in the words of writer Red Kelly.

It was 1964, and little Leighton was a huge deal. Another kid who hung out at Singing Cloud rehearsals when he wasn't playing baseball with cousin Jimmy Hughes started asking for his own introduction to Rick Hall. Singer Percy Sledge had previously failed to get a meeting with James Joiner of Tune. Instead, Joiner had stood with Sledge on the public sidewalk

Recorded at Norala Studios in 1966, Percy Sledge's "When a Man Loves a Woman" was a #1 R&B and pop hit. Sledge grew up just outside of Muscle Shoals and captured the town's first #1 hit.

outside his office to say he didn't understand what Sledge was doing. Sledge recorded a demo at FAME, but Hall passed. Sledge then turned to Quin Ivy, a DJ and songwriter who in 1965 was soft-launching a studio he would call Norala. Working with FAME house regulars Roger Hawkins on drums, Spooner Oldham on Farfisa organ, Junior Lowe on bass, and Marlin Greene on guitar, they recorded a tune Sledge and Greene had worked on, "When a Man Loves a Woman."

The song's descending chords rippled with heat, while Greene's least-possible guitar lines flickered like sparks in vast emotional space. "When a Man Loves a Woman" bled truth, and Hall knew it. He phoned Atlantic Records gatekeeper Jerry Wexler while Wexler was having a pool party in Great Neck, Long Island, telling him act now and you can have a hit on your hands. Soon "When a Man Loves a Woman" topped *Billboard*'s Hot 100 and the R&B charts in 1966.

The song was "wrong" in fetching ways: the horns a little out of tune, Sledge himself just standing on a mark, singing the loud and soft parts without ever changing how close he was to the mic. The engineer—predicting where the vocal would go next—twirled the knob to compensate. It worked.

"I had a lot of strong feelings about country and R&B being interrelated," keyboardist Spooner Oldham told Barney Hoskyns later. "Percy was a country singer, in a sense. I can hear that nasal country sound in his voice even now. He had that more than most *country* singers."

The success of Alexander, Hughes, Sledge, and all that was coming out of the Shoals over the next few years rippled through America. It brought Jerry Wexler and Rick Hall into collaboration—and heading toward a life-changing collision. It shaped what America thought Black voices sounded like, and, though it was not well-known at the time, showed that white and Black people could make art together. In his memoir of America in the 1960s, Alabama historian Frye Gaillard describes the era as a "time of tension in which . . . there was a little oasis in Northern Alabama. Nobody could quite say why it was there. Maybe it was just the blind luck of history. But in the nearly contiguous small towns of Florence, Muscle Shoals, Tuscumbia, and Sheffield . . . there was a place where music was an antidote to prejudice."

Well, *maybe?* But the story of Arthur Alexander offers alternate ways of assessing things. The guys up at Stafford's Spar studio

OPPOSITE PAGE: These leather shoes were worn by Percy Sledge.

ARTIFACT COURTESY OF THE ALABAMA MUSIC HALL OF FAME

ABOVE: In 1966, the National Association of Radio Announcers presented this Golden Mike Award for Single Record of the Year to Percy Sledge for "When a Man Loves a Woman."

ARTIFACT COURTESY OF THE ALABAMA MUSIC HALL OF FAME

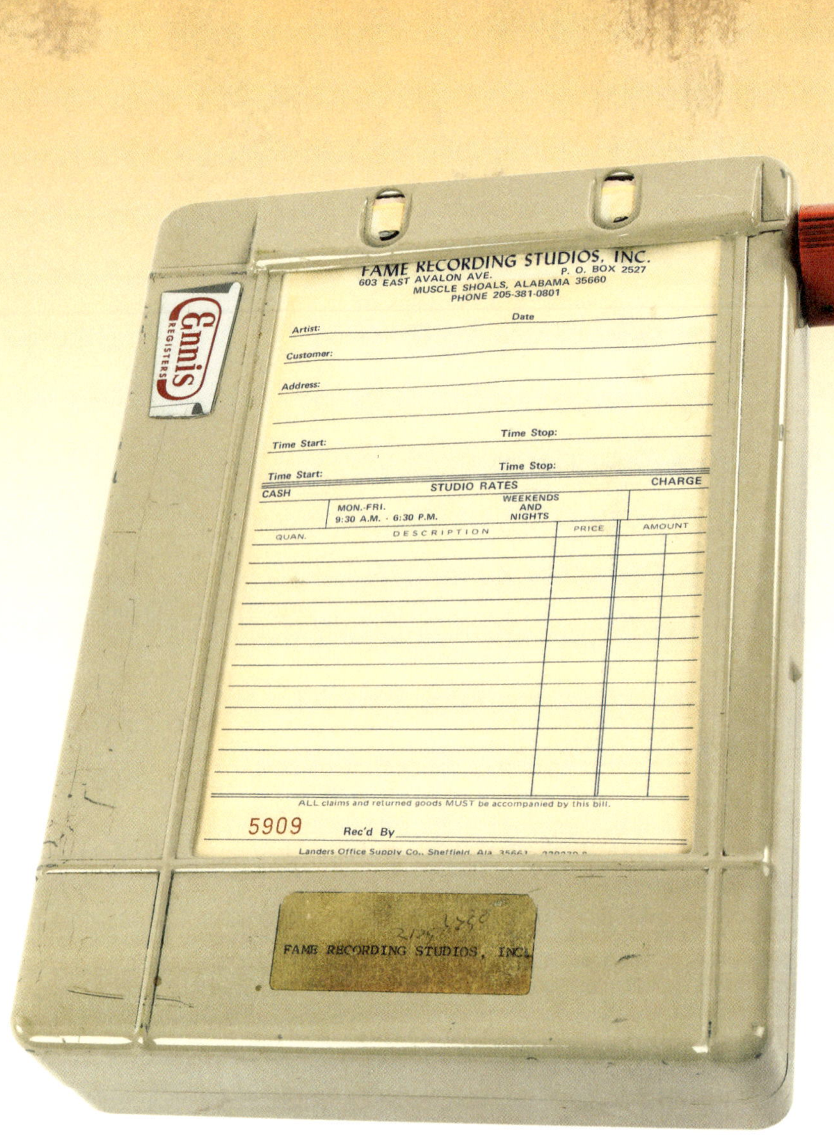

could proudly declare "we didn't see color." Some of them had never sat in a room next to a Black person; whatever they expected, Alexander was his own person. He of course knew far more clearly the lines between them.

He had powerful fans—the Beatles, Stones, Dylan—and many more who only loved his voice. But Arthur Alexander struggled through life and that is his story, too. If the early days of rock & roll displayed an amazing lack of safety features that made what followed possible, they also ensured that the Black artist thrown out in front of white audiences had a life-sized target sewn on their back.

Backup was in short supply. In Alexander's near future, the material he sang was sometimes less than stellar, the recordings uneven. Money disappeared, and he began to display the effects of substance addictions and physical and mental afflictions. He experienced treatment in institutions both correctional and medical that did not help him. He left the music business behind, drove a bus in Cleveland, and was making a small, hopeful return to form late in life when he died of a heart attack in Nashville in 1993.

This invoice register machine was used by Rick Hall for FAME sessions in the 1960s.

ARTIFACT COURTESY OF THE ROCK & ROLL HALL OF FAME

OPPOSITE PAGE: TOP ROW, FROM LEFT: Barry Beckett, Aaron Varnell, Jimmy Johnson, unidentified, Roger Hawkins, Mickey Buckins, and David Hood.
BOTTOM ROW, FROM LEFT: Charlie Chalmers, unidentified, Gene "Bowlegs" Miller, and James Mitchell, c. late 1960s.

PHOTO COURTESY OF FAME RECORDING STUDIOS

Donnie Fritts, a studio musician and songwriter who remained a lifelong friend, saw more nuance than most. "I had people asking me why we were 'fooling with n----rs,'" he told writer Barney Hoskyns. "We were so visible, right in the middle of Florence above that drugstore, with Arthur and his friends coming in and out all day. The whole town hated it."

Hall would keep photographers out of FAME, and he would ask musicians to park their cars away from the studio, so that people—white people in particular—would not know when they were recording at FAME. Maybe it wasn't that the Shoals scene thrived despite the fact that a lot of outsiders never knew what was going on. Perhaps it thrived because so few knew anything but the luminous music it brought to the world.

Asked once for his definition of a crucial word in the Muscle Shoals lexicon, Dan Penn tossed off what *funk* meant to him. "Funk is anything that you ain't supposed to do . . . but you can get away with," he said. Muscle Shoals brought forth the sound of a lot of people slipping the path that life had in store for them. Getting away with something huge.

IN THE middle OF IT ALL

BY PATTERSON HOOD

Muscle Shoals was such a weird place to grow up because it's the most unlikely place on earth for what happened.

Let me set the scene. In the northwest corner of Alabama, there are four towns, three of which—Sheffield, Tuscumbia, and Muscle Shoals—sit nearly connected on the south side of the Tennessee River with only a sign to tell you when you have left one and entered the other. The fourth one, Florence, sits on the north side of the river. It is the biggest of the four towns, although the combined population of the entire metropolitan area is barely 200,000. That is probably close to twice what the population was back in the '70s and '80s when I was growing up there. The entire region is better known as the Muscle Shoals area (or the Quad Cities).

Although it has come a long way, inching toward some sort of progress, the Shoals area that I grew up in consisted of two "dry" counties (Lauderdale and Colbert), meaning that to buy a beer you either went to a bootlegger or drove fifteen miles to the Tennessee state line, where you could find a few package stores and honky-tonks. To buy liquor you had to drive a good bit farther, an hour, to the closest towns that sold such things. Or, go to the bootlegger, of which there were many.

David Hood of the Swampers, and his son, Patterson Hood, of the Drive-By Truckers, pose with the custom-built Gibson "Alabama Jammer" guitar, c. 2010.
PHOTO COURTESY OF DAVID AND JUDY HOOD

Patterson Hood acquired this Seagull S6 acoustic guitar soon after moving to Athens, Georgia, and he used it to write all his Drive-By Truckers songs from 1995 to 2003.

ARTIFACT COURTESY OF PATTERSON HOOD

My hometown was the kind of deeply conservative place where, upon meeting someone new, often the first question asked was, "What church do you go to?" The Shoals area was as Bible Belt as it got, essentially controlled by the Church of Christ, politically and socially. They worked hard to keep progressive ideas (on race, or gender, or sexuality), liquor, and any semblance of fun at bay.

It was also the home of a musical miracle. Between 1965 and 1982, hundreds of records were cut in Muscle Shoals at one or more of the several studios scattered around. Many of those records became hits, which led to an amazing array of major artists coming to my sleepy hometown to record at one of the humble little recording studios that had popped up there in the wake of a couple of regional soul hits that had come from FAME Studio. My dad, David Hood, was in the middle of it all, because he played bass in a core group of session players at FAME and then at Muscle Shoals Sound Studio. So I was in the middle of it all, too.

Of course, this is in the heart of the civil rights-era Alabama, with white musicians backing Black artists—Aretha Franklin, Wilson Pickett, Percy Sledge, and many more. So it's a miraculous story on so many levels. But when I was growing up, I learned early not to talk about it at school. I was in second grade with Roger Hawkins's son Dale. And one day at school, when we're doing show & tell in front of the class, he was talking about his dad being the greatest drummer in the world. And I knew my dad just had to be the greatest bass player.

Patterson and David Hood onstage with the Drive-By Truckers in 2010. PHOTO COURTESY OF DAVID AND JUDY HOOD

But on the school playground that wasn't totally appreciated. I made a mental note to myself at age seven. It's like, "Oh, at school we don't talk about what dad does." And so most of my friends had no idea what my dad was doing. And most of the locals at that time had no idea what was going on in the studios. I think the musicians wanted to keep it underground because they were afraid people would stop them from doing it. They were having fun, and they didn't want to be stopped. Just having beer in the studio was potentially something they could get in trouble for because it was a dry county. So it was a strange dynamic at work that maybe made it better.

My dad worked crazy hours because they would start a session at noon. That meant Dad was there by 10 o'clock because he's always early. Anybody who knows my dad knows that "on time" for him is two hours early. And then he wouldn't get home until after I was in bed. But he made a point of getting up every morning and fixing me breakfast, so we could sit and enjoy it together.

This 1957 Fender Precision bass was played by David Hood at recording sessions between 1976 and 1988.

ARTIFACT COURTESY OF DAVID HOOD

And I would just bombard him with questions about what he was working on, and he would try not to answer. He didn't want to really give me a lot of info. I'd say to him: "I heard Rod Stewart's in town. How's it going?" And he would just say, "Oh, it's fine."

Still, I became obsessed with what was happening in the local studios. But I didn't really get to go very often. And Jimmy Johnson's son Jay, he would get to go to the studio a lot. And Jay was my age. He was like a year younger, but we grew up around each other some. So then I'd be talking to Jay on the phone, and he would tell me, "Oh, I got to watch Mark Knopfler playing lead on such and such song." And I would just go, "What?!" And I'd be thinking, "Damn it, Dad!" But that's just the way it was.

So it was a rare occasion that I really got to meet the artists and musicians who came through town. But the exceptions are kind of exceptional. Linda Ronstadt came to Muscle Shoals to record, making her third album. She was on tour with the Eagles backing her up, and they came through Muscle Shoals on a day or two off, in the middle of the tour. They were all there, but she recorded with the Muscle Shoals Rhythm Section. Somehow Linda ended up at our house, and she and my mom really hit it off. I have this incredible memory being about six years old and sitting on a waterbed with Linda Ronstadt, and her talking to me, reading me a bedtime story, and tucking me in.

Then, when she became one of the biggest stars in the world, some years later, she was touring and she routed her tour to play in Florence, and played at the University of North Alabama.

Mike Cooley and Patterson Hood of the Drive-By Truckers accompany Bettye LaVette while recording her 2007 album, *The Scene of the Crime*, at FAME. The record was co-produced by Patterson Hood. PHOTO COURTESY OF BETTYE LAVETTE AND KEVIN KILEY

And by then I was twelve, and I was very smitten with Linda Ronstadt like any twelve-year-old boy in 1975 would have been. We all got to go to the concert, which was great in itself. But then I came home from school, and Linda was sitting in our den, hanging out with Mom. What a mind-blowing time.

I've spent my whole life obsessed with Muscle Shoals, with the music and with what happened there. I call it "The Miracle Story." And as much as I lived it and know about it, I still don't fully understand how it happened and how come it happened there. Some folks say that radio station WLAY, which served that whole area, planted the seeds. Because WLAY played R&B music, country music, early rock & roll, Top Forty hits, and bubble gum pop. They played everything, the kind of diverse playlist that didn't occur on radio for years after that.

Those young musicians, who became the core of the Muscle Shoals recording scene, grew up listening to an incredible variety of music on WLAY. So when they started learning to play, they naturally tried all kinds of different stuff. And so that might be some part of why it happened there. And of course, some people say it's all because of the Tennessee River, "the singing river." I really don't know why Muscle Shoals became such an amazing music center, but I'm so glad I grew up in the middle of it all.

THAT'S HOW THEY GOT TO NASHVILLE:
THE ORIGINAL MUSCLE SHOALS

rhythm section

BY WARREN DENNEY

Rick Hall and FAME's original rhythm section had that fire in the belly—all young men, wrestling for love, music, money, and survival.

Three members in particular—bassist Norbert Putnam, keys player David Briggs, and drummer Jerry Carrigan—held it down for Hall in the beginning, underpinning a wealth of R&B and rock & roll recordings coming out of Hall's FAME Studio between 1960 and 1964, the year the three moved north to Nashville.

That trio conjured sounds that would affect the course of R&B, rock & roll, and country music permanently. Along the way, they broadened the scope of Nashville music, opening the door to a more diverse range of artists.

"The most important development in country music history, between Elvis and Garth, was the arrival in Nashville of the original Muscle Shoals rhythm section," music writer David Cantwell said in *Heartaches by the Number: Country Music's 500 Greatest Singles*. "After bassist Norbert Putnam, pianist

The original Muscle Shoals Rhythm Section and others with singer Tommy Roe at a c. 1963 recording session.
FROM LEFT: Rick Hall, Felton Jarvis, Tommy Roe, Ray Stevens, David Briggs, Norbert Putnam, and Jerry Carrigan (bottom). PHOTO COURTESY OF FAME RECORDING STUDIOS

Musician and producer Norbert Putnam played this 1965 Fender Precision bass on hundreds of recordings, including releases by Joan Baez, Elvis Presley, Linda Ronstadt, and Tony Joe White.

ARTIFACT COURTESY OF NORBERT PUTNAM

David Briggs, and drummer Jerry Carrigan left Alabama for Nashville in late 1964, they anchored a second-generation A-Team that would help fashion a new soul-and-pop-inflected country music."

Prior to working for Hall, the three honed their chops in local Shoals bands: the Rhythm Rockets, the Mark V, and Dan Penn & the Pallbearers. They covered Elvis, rock & roll, and R&B, playing for kids in gymnasiums and fraternity dance parties across the state.

The cadre formed a relationship with the manager of the Princess Theater in Florence, Tom Stafford, and spent hours above the City Drug Store cutting demos for Spar Music (Stafford Publishing and Recording). Aspiring songwriters, musicians, and producers including Hall, Penn, Billy Sherrill, Spooner Oldham, and Donnie Fritts were among future heavyweights who would visit Spar. Then a catalyst arrived.

"The thing that changed everything was the day Arthur Alexander showed up upstairs at the drug store," Putnam said.

Meanwhile, a crucial business was forming. FAME publishing was founded in 1959 by Hall, Sherrill, and Stafford, with sole ownership going to Hall in 1960. He found warehouse space in a row of buildings Henry Ford had built, cleaned it up, and fashioned a rudimentary control room on the site. His first order of business was to produce Alexander, a promising local singer and songwriter.

"We went over to the warehouse, and Rick had a four-channel mixer," Putnam said. "He had Terry Thompson there. Terry was the greatest guitar player in Muscle Shoals at the time. He was an old guy—might have been twenty-four. Carrigan is seventeen, I'm eighteen, and Briggs is eighteen.

"We only did three songs with Arthur, and he's on one side singing and on the other side, there's Peanutt Montgomery [also in Hall's original rhythm section] standing on some Coca-Cola crates to get his guitar up, even with the other side of the mic, and Rick would move him back and move him back until he had a balance on the vocal and the guitar. It's four mics. And I'll tell you, if you listen to the original recording of 'You Better Move On,' it's well-balanced, it's a good mix. It wasn't easy to do."

"You Better Move On" was released on Dot Records late in 1961 after Hall came to Nashville and shopped the three sides around. The indie label had connections to WLAC radio in town, one of the most powerful R&B platforms in the U.S. Unimaginably, "You Better Move On" hit #24 on the pop charts. The release of the record, along with the B-side "A Shot of Rhythm and Blues," written by Thompson, was a watershed moment for the Muscle Shoals scene.

FAME was on the map. Briggs, Carrigan, and Putnam would soon find themselves on hit records by Jimmy Hughes ("Steal Away"), the Tams ("What Kind of Fool Do You Think I Am"), Joe Tex ("Hold What You've Got"), and several by Tommy Roe. After conversations with Nashville up-and-comers Bob Beckham and Ray Stevens, who had also produced and recorded in Muscle Shoals, the trio began to think about Nashville seriously. Stevens told them they could make real money.

"It was starting to make sense," Putnam recalled. "[Ray Stevens] said, 'You play the young music with a lot of feel. Do you have any idea how much money you'd be making if you were doing these sessions in Nashville?' I think the scale had moved up to $50, and he said if we found a groove, we could make $200 in a day with four sessions. That's $1,000 a week. I'd made $10,000 for the whole previous year. That's more money than God makes!"

As they soon were to find out, what they thought was a liability—being R&B and rock & roll players in a country world—was actually their superpower. Veteran session ace Harold Bradley later told Putnam that it was a regular topic of conversation at music insider parties in Nashville that there was a need to broaden the scope of the town's music. "He said Ray would always come back from Muscle Shoals and was very big on us," Putnam said. "We were on the radar and in their thoughts. . . . They thought we could make it, and they put us in the demo routine to see if we got better, and we did."

The experiment took root, and flourished, informing country music along the way. Putnam, Briggs, and Carrigan not only became first-call session players in Nashville, but rose to become producers, studio owners, and publishers who would leave an indelible mark on country and popular music.

WHEN SKYDOG MET

wicked pickett

MAKING A SAD SONG (WAY) BETTER

BY MICHAEL A. GONZALES

On November 27, 1968, singer Wilson Pickett was working on his eighth studio album at his favorite sound lab, FAME Studio in Muscle Shoals. A Southern soul sensation signed to Atlantic Records, he had rocked radio and shaken stages throughout the decade. That day in Muscle Shoals, Pickett didn't have any ideas, but session guitarist Duane Allman suggested they try remaking the Beatles' recent hit "Hey Jude."

It was an audacious suggestion because the record had just ended its nine-week run at #1 as of the November 9 *Billboard* chart. The song was still all over the radio. Pickett was skeptical at first, but what began as a goof between a Black singer, a hillbilly hippie guitarist, and studio owner-producer Rick Hall became legendary.

Though the man some called "Wicked Pickett" appeared in the excellent 2013 documentary *Muscle Shoals* and has had a brilliant biography written about him (2017's *In the Midnight Hour* by Tony Fletcher), there hasn't been much documentation on the vocalist who was once the biggest act on Atlantic. With hits that included "In the Midnight Hour," "Land of 1000 Dances," and "Funky Broadway," Pickett created high expectations that "Hey Jude" too would join them in the upper reaches of the charts. It didn't.

The single came right as Atlantic was releasing Led Zeppelin's debut, signaling a shift in label priorities. The album *Hey Jude* wasn't Pickett's swan song from the company (there would be three more albums), but it's considered one of the last successful

Wilson Pickett at FAME Studio, 1968. PHOTO COURTESY OF FAME RECORDING STUDIOS

ABOVE: Built in 1964, this was one of two sunburst-finish Fender Stratocasters used by Duane Allman when he was a session musician at FAME and Muscle Shoals Sound Studio, from 1968 to 1969. ARTIFACT COURTESY OF MICKEY BUCKINS

OPPOSITE PAGE: Wilson Pickett and Duane Allman at FAME, 1968. MICHAEL OCHS ARCHIVES/GETTY IMAGES

Southern soul discs in a changing musical era. Pickett left Atlantic after 1971's *Don't Knock My Love*, but would still return to Muscle Shoals to lay down soul with the Swampers.

Pickett first came to FAME in 1966 after having recorded his breakthrough pop and R&B hits at the Stax studio in Memphis. The studio switch was a choice made by Atlantic producer Jerry Wexler. "Most of our artists like to record hot Southern style and they simply couldn't go through the Broadway changes in New York," he told *Hit Parader* in 1970. "The word was blowing North about this funky little studio in a place called Muscle Shoals, so I took Wilson Pickett down there. It was just incredible. The musicians were out of sight, [playing with] raw feeling."

On his first day there in May 1966, Pickett was a bit confused by what Rick Hall and the all-white Muscle Shoals Rhythm Section could offer. Yet once they were settled and began recording the riotous "Land of 1000 Dances," the singer knew he was in the right place.

Born and raised 200 miles away in Prattville, Alabama, Pickett didn't have many pleasant memories of growing up down south. The fourth of eleven kids, he was abandoned by his father, endured physical abuse from his mother, and dreamed of the day when he could escape the cotton fields.

Pickett's one solace was singing in the church choir with sister Jeannie. Tony Fletcher wrote, "On Sunday mornings the pair would break into gospel hymns as they wended through the

woods on a short cut down to Jericho Baptist, provoking holy shouts from the porches of the other sharecropping shacks where folks were busy readying themselves for the Sunday service."

A few years later, he was singing in various gospel quartets. When he was a teenager, he went to Detroit, where his father lived with a new wife, and got a taste of the music business. In 1955, he joined forces with gospel singers the Violinaires, but five years later hooked up with another group, the Falcons.

Pickett had also grown disillusioned with church folks he encountered who were just as devilish as the people they railed against. He claimed when he sang at C. L. Franklin's church in Detroit that some of the parishioners were intoxicated. "I might as well be singing rock & roll as singing to a drunken audience," he told his sister Bretha. "I might as well make some money."

In Detroit, Pickett developed into a gritty-voiced singer. James Brown once hired the young singer's group the Falcons as an

Wilson Pickett's recording of John Lennon and Paul McCartney's "Hey Jude" was a pop and R&B hit in 1968.

ARTIFACT COURTESY OF FAME RECORDING STUDIOS

OPPOSITE PAGE: Session drummer Johnny Sandlin and guitarist Duane Allman recording at FAME, 1968.

PHOTO COURTESY OF FAME RECORDING STUDIOS

opening act and then kicked them off the tour, because Pickett's soul shouts were louder than his.

Usually when Pickett went to FAME to record, Jerry Wexler was producing, the sessions were planned, and the material was already chosen. When Pickett arrived in Alabama for the November 1968 sessions, Wexler couldn't leave New York. The show went on with Rick Hall producing, even if it did take a few detours.

Duane Allman wasn't a regular session guitarist at FAME, but after hanging around the studio in the summer of '68, he finally got some session work. The year before, Duane and younger brother Gregg recorded there with their band Hour Glass.

The Allmans had been living in Los Angeles and recorded two albums for Liberty Records (1967's *Hour Glass* and 1968's *Power of Love*). On *Power of Love*, which was engineered by Muscle Shoals guitarist Jimmy Johnson, the brothers remade the Beatles' "Norwegian Wood (This Bird Has Flown)," a song they performed live. Few Hour Glass albums were sold, and the group was dropped from Liberty and eventually disbanded.

Allman packed his many guitars and drove to Alabama looking for work. Rick Hall told him straight up, "Duane, I have six guitar players. . . . I don't have a place for you." But Allman kept hanging around, and on November 12, 1968, he chipped in some tasty slide guitar work on Clarence Carter's "Road of Love." That session was Duane's way of showing Hall and the Swampers what he could do. Two weeks later, he really showed them.

In those days, folks at FAME called Duane Allman by his nickname, Dog, which he embraced fully. However, because of his close relationship with uplifting stimulants, Allman's new buddy Wilson Pickett called him Skyman. It wasn't long before someone put the monikers together and began calling him Skydog.

Pickett and Allman felt like outcasts in Muscle Shoals, where conservative white residents didn't generally take kindly to Black visitors or hippies. Pickett and Allman weren't exactly the type of person who would be accepted with a smile at local restaurants. They stayed at the studio while the rest of the musicians went to a diner, and it was then that Allman persuaded Pickett that "Hey Jude" should be their next challenge. When the other musicians returned, they were surprised to be asked to set aside the morning's tracks for later. "Hey Jude" was up next. Ever the professionals, they jumped into the fire. What began as a small flame became a blazing inferno.

"Allman was unusual among contemporary session guitarists in that he played his instrument, a Fender Stratocaster, standing up, as if on stage," his biographer Fletcher wrote. "Pickett would have it no other way for his own part—and the moment they hit the coda, Pickett unleashed a primal scream that led into a high-pitched holler and the two locked into a musical communication that took on a lifeforce of its own."

After capturing lightning in a bottle, Hall called Wexler and blasted "Hey Jude" over the phone. Excited, Wexler put a rush on getting the single pressed and released; it was in stores two months later, though it peaked modestly at #23 pop and #13 on the R&B charts. Nevertheless, Wexler inquired about the guitar player, whose contract he later bought. In an era when the session musicians were mostly anonymous, it wasn't long before Allman's work with Pickett had the industry buzzing. He and that Strat appeared on records by Aretha Franklin ("The Weight"), King Curtis ("Games People Play"), Boz Scaggs ("Loan Me a Dime"), Derek & the Dominos ("Layla"), and a few others wanting some of that Skydog seasoning on their projects.

Allman's electric blues slide guitar on "Hey Jude" also helped lay the foundation for the Southern rock of the Allman Brothers Band, a group he formed with brother Gregg in 1969. Jimmy Johnson told *Mojo* magazine in 2002, "Duane's whole career spun off that Pickett session; it's amazing how one incident, one session, can change a person's life." In England, Pickett's cover of "Hey Jude" was a smash. One fan was Tom Jones, who often thought of himself as "the white Wilson Pickett." From 1969 to 1971, Jones had a prime-time ABC-TV variety show called *This Is Tom Jones*, and he invited Pickett to appear. Together they sang a medley of Pickett's singles, including "Barefootin'," "In the Midnight Hour," and "Hey Jude."

In Jones's autobiography, *Over the Top and Back*, he recalled, "We had done this blistering duet on 'Hey Jude,' pushing each other all the way, having a great time, ending up in each other's arms at the end of it—one of those duets where it feels so good you just have to laugh."

Pickett continued to record and tour, but his last years were a mixture of joy and misery. In 1991, he was inducted into the Rock & Roll Hall of Fame. He later spent time in jail for waving his shotgun at people and threatening the mayor of Englewood, New Jersey. He also dealt with numerous illnesses and ailments but refused to slow down until he had no choice. On January 19, 2006, Wilson Pickett died at the age of sixty-four. In his lifetime he created a few eternal classics at Muscle Shoals, and the rocking soul of "Hey Jude" belongs on top of the heap.

OPPOSITE PAGE BOTTOM: Bobby Womack, Wilson Pickett, and Jimmy Johnson recording at FAME, 1968. Womack wrote several songs recorded by Pickett, including the 1968 hit "I'm in Love."

PHOTO COURTESY OF FAME RECORDING STUDIOS

RIGHT: Wilson Pickett wore this jumpsuit on the cover of his 1971 album *The Best of Wilson Pickett Vol. II* (opposite, top). The album included Pickett's version of the Beatles' "Hey Jude"

ARTIFACT COURTESY OF THE ROCK & ROLL HALL OF FAME

SWEET FEELINGS & HOME-GROWN VEGETABLES: THE NECESSITY OF

candi staton

BY FRANCESCA ROYSTER

Candi Staton's voice holds sweet heat like an ember, glowing, a hint of ash of past pain around its edges. Hers is the voice of resilience. And that voice came into its own when she arrived at FAME in 1968, recording some of her best work, including her trademark tender-yet-funky covers of country songs like "Stand by Your Man" (1971), "In the Ghetto" (1972), and "Jolene" (recorded in 1974 and released in 2011).

Like her friend and confidant Ray Charles, she makes music that fluidly crosses genre lines, helping us hear the gospel in blues, the blues in country, the country soul in R&B, and the twinning double-helix vibrations of disco and house. "I've always been a little stubborn with my music," she said. "They try to put me in a genre, and I won't go. If I don't feel it, I won't do it. I have to feel what I sing." Candi has made music that is both memorable and meaningful during some of our nation's most difficult eras. Recording with some of the best producers and session musicians of the 1970s and 1980s, she has repeatedly defied the music industry's genre-driven racial segregation.

The daughter of a hard-working, hard-drinking coal miner father who was sometimes violent, and a religious mother who

Candi Staton poses in a striking fur coat at FAME, c. 1969. PHOTO COURTESY OF FAME RECORDING STUDIOS

knew how to survive, Canzetta Maria Staton grew up in Hanceville, Alabama, just seventy-five miles from Muscle Shoals. She was raised on a diet of beans, rice, and home-grown vegetables, as well as country and gospel music and the occasional blues song. Like her contemporaries Aretha Franklin and Mavis Staples, Candi Staton earned early recognition for singing in church (though she views her voice as a gift from God, rather than the product of her considerable individual talent). At age eleven, she was invited to tour as a part of the Jewell Gospel Trio, and recorded for Nashboro, Apollo, and Savoy Records in the 1950s under the direction of mentor Nettie Mae Harrison. During her career as a young gospel singer, harmonizing with her sister Maggie and bandmate Naomi Harrison, Candi learned many lessons that would shape her career, including how to tell a story in a way that captures the experiences of the sinner and the sinned upon. Most of all, she used her voice to work and to survive. She told me, "You asked what helped me know that music was going to be my passion and life's work? *Necessity*. I had no choice." After years of touring with the Jewell Gospel Trio and never being paid except for room and board, Candi returned home and found work performing in local clubs and the Chitlin' Circuit. In the meantime, she had four children and a difficult, violent marriage she survived and escaped.

Candi Staton wore this custom-made buckskin jacket and pants, embellished with feathers and leather fringe, in the 1970s.
ARTIFACT COURTESY OF CANDI STATON

OPPOSITE PAGE: Session musicians Clayton Ivey and Bob Wray accompany Candi Staton at FAME, c. 1970. PHOTO COURTESY OF FAME RECORDING STUDIOS

She first recorded for FAME Records on September 25, 1968, which yielded her first single, "I'd Rather Be an Old Man's Sweetheart (Than a Young Man's Fool)." She was introduced to producer Rick Hall by musician and her eventual husband Clarence Carter. Candi had been an opening act for Carter when she was playing clubs in Alabama, and Carter knew that Hall would hear in her voice the power that he heard. "When I auditioned for Rick, he signed me that same night, and the rest is history," she said.

At FAME, Hall had gathered a band of savvy musicians to create a sound sturdy and also pliable enough to support Candi, Aretha, and Etta, too. Over the years, folks have struggled to define that sound, made by mostly white and a few Black musicians in the segregated South. Maybe the sound of Muscle Shoals is an embodied collective knowledge, the reflection of contentious history held in the water of the nearby Tennessee River, since, as Toni Morrison has said, "Water has a perfect memory and is forever trying to get back to where it was."

Perhaps that water remembers what it feels like to grow up both together and apart, Black, brown, and white, the places where people touched, came together and sometimes hurt each other. Candi's father and the other Alabama miners, returning from the

Candi Staton was among the performers at the annual ShoalsFest, held at McFarland Park, Florence, Alabama, October 2021.

ARTIFACT COURTESY OF CANDI STATON

OPPOSITE PAGE: Candi Staton poses with (CLOCKWISE FROM BOTTOM LEFT) FAME Studios owner Rick Hall, Warner Brothers Records executive John Salstone, musicians David Hood and Barry Beckett, and musician Randy McCormick, 1974.

PHOTO BY DICK COOPER

BOTTOM: Candi Staton in the vocal booth at FAME, c. 1970.

PHOTO COURTESY OF FAME RECORDING STUDIOS

bowels of the earth, lungs heavy with the dust of rock and earth. The cotton fields that were once visible from the front door of FAME, and the fingers that picked them. Strikes and boycotts. Lynchings and race riots. George Wallace, holding watch at the schoolhouse door. The crimson in the tide. But this was also the state that birthed and raised Rosa Parks, Coretta Scott King, John Lewis, the seat of the Civil Rights Movement. In this music, you can hear the precarious coming together of people despite that tough history. Its soulfulness might well be a result of those tensions, the "old deep down, coming out of your stomach, coming out of your gut" feeling, as Candi described it. Love and terror both, pushed under until it eddies back up again. What else to do but turn it into the pulse of bass, the pop of drums, the broken chords of a keyboard powerful enough to summon church, and steady enough to hold and carry the wails of Percy Sledge, the get over here and tell mama authority of Etta James, the warm and worldly life knowledge of Candi Staton?

In even her most danceable music, Candi has the voice of someone who has found a hidden source of strength. Her voice is clear, even in its expression of complicated feelings. When she gives advice, it often comes with a chuckle, cut with the wisdom of hard-won experience, as when she confesses in "I'd Rather Be an Old Man's Sweetheart (Than a Young Man's Fool)":

Most girls prefer a young man
'Cause a young man is strong
But I'd rather put up with this old man
Than have a young man doing me wrong.

Sometimes the song is a lesson in process. In her 1971 version of "Stand by Your Man," those heartfelt "mmmm hmms" tell you just as much as the advice "to give him something, something warm to cling to." In "Jolene," her cover of Dolly Parton's song recorded just a few months after Parton's, though unreleased until 2011, Candi does not beg, she *warns*: "I'm telling you, don't you take my man." (In contrast with Dolly's heartbreak, Candi expresses a strength and decisiveness foreshadowing Beyoncé's 2024 "Jolene." I'm sure Beyoncé was inspired by it.) In her 1976 disco hit "Young Hearts Run Free," written by David Crawford after Candi shared her experience of fleeing domestic violence, she lays out her truth directly, right in those opening lines: "What's the sense in sharing this one and only life / Ending up just another lost and lonely wife?"

Candi reflected on the song's continued impact: "The good thing is, the young people are getting the words now. At first they were just listening to the beat—you put 'Young Hearts Run Free' on at the club, and the whole dance floor fills up. But they don't know they're dancing to a sad song. But then they listen to the lyrics and they just realize, 'Now I know what my mother was listening to in the kitchen when she was cooking breakfast and I danced with her and didn't know what I was dancing to. Now I do. I'm forty and it's happening to me.'" Candi Staton's sense of purpose—whether she's singing a love song, a dance song, or a spiritual; whether country, soul, or disco—is what keeps us listening, and digging into the truths beneath the lyrics. It's what helps us find our own story in hers.

bobbie gentry

SO CLOSE TO HOME

BY STEPHEN DEUSNER

Muscle Shoals must have felt like home to Bobbie Gentry. She was born and raised in Chickasaw County, Mississippi, just two hours away but somehow even more rural, even more *country* than the Shoals. Her childhood was spent on her grandparents' farm, which had no electricity or running water, but she later regarded it as idyllic nevertheless.

Even after she moved to Los Angeles at thirteen years old, Gentry would plumb her memories of home for inspiration. "Ode to Billie Joe," her breakthrough single and a #1 pop hit in 1967, recounted a dinner table conversation about a small-town scandal, and her finest album, 1968's *The Delta Sweete*, depicts the South through her warmly observant lyrics, vivid arrangements, and wild sound collages. The South as it sat in her memory was always her primary subject, although until 1969 she had never actually recorded there.

By then, Gentry's career had grown precarious. "Ode to Billie Joe" was a massive hit, but subsequent singles and albums missed the charts. Her collection of duets with Glen Campbell sold well and won them Grammys, but most of the credit went to him, not her. As a live act, however, Gentry was thriving. She had an ongoing residency at the Landmark Hotel in Las Vegas, where she controlled nearly every aspect of the show: she wrote and produced the music, devised the staging and the choreography, and even designed the costumes. When she took breaks from that tiring engagement, Gentry traveled back to Chickasaw County, where she stayed with her grandparents and ate lots of home cooking.

Rick Hall, the mastermind at FAME Studios, saw what was absent from Gentry's underperforming singles and what she needed to have another hit: the South. In his autobiography *The Man from Muscle Shoals: My Journey from Shame to FAME*, he recalls driving to the studio and hearing "Ode to Billie Joe" on the radio and nearly crashing his car. He was struck by her sophisticated storytelling and her eye for details that only a real Southerner would know—one who had known rural poverty as he had. In her music he recognized his own experiences growing up in remote Freedom Hills, Alabama, and he was determined to bring Gentry to FAME to cut a record. When she did agree to collaborate, he challenged her to write something akin to "Billie Joe," a narrative full of realistic characters and a Southern setting. Gentry responded by looking over the many short stories she had written but not published. One in particular stood out as a potential pop song—an intensely southern gothic tale about the dark goings-on in a poor family. When she read Hall the lyrics over the phone, it took more than ten minutes. Cut out the incest, violence, and sex, he said, and it should come in under five minutes.

Bobbie Gentry at FAME, recording her sixth studio album, *Fancy*, c. 1969.
Rick Hall likened producing the album to "producing a movie score" because it painted "a picture in your mind." PHOTO COURTESY OF FAME RECORDING STUDIOS

January 4, 1978

Dear Linda and Rick,

You have been such kind and gracious hosts, and we have enjoyed our stay in your lovely home so much. You have shown us the true southern hospitality in its finest sense, and we will always remember our stay with you and your family, with the fondest of memories.

Thank you for everything—

Bobbie Gentry

Bobbie Gentry wrote this note to Rick and Linda Hall, thanking them for allowing her to stay in the artist guest house on their ranch, 1978. ARTIFACT COURTESY OF FAME RECORDING STUDIOS

OPPOSITE PAGE: Bobbie Gentry talks with FAME session musicians, c. 1969. PHOTO COURTESY OF FAME RECORDING STUDIOS

BOTTOM: Muscle Shoals Rhythm Section guitarist Junior Lowe shares a lighthearted moment with Bobbie Gentry at FAME, c. 1969. PHOTO COURTESY OF FAME RECORDING STUDIOS

Gentry arrived in Muscle Shoals by private jet, sporting a massive five-carat diamond ring—both gifts from her soon-to-be husband, William Harrah of Harrah's Casino. At FAME, she cut the new track with members of the FAME Gang (who had replaced the Swampers when they opened their own studio earlier that year). Hall flew the masters out to Las Vegas to record backing vocals by the Sweet Inspirations (which included Cissy Houston). Then he hired Jimmie Haskell to write string arrangements as distinctive as the one he contributed to "Ode to Billie Joe." Hall was determined to get it just right, ultimately creating 167 mixes before settling on the right one. "To me, producing 'Fancy' was like producing a movie score," Hall wrote. "I wanted to take her sound one step further. I wanted every sound on the record to make listeners visualize the lyrics. I wanted the record to be as deep and dirty as the Mississippi Delta and as dark and twisted as 'Tobacco Road.'"

Funky yet cinematic, the arrangement tells as much of the story as the lyrics do. Gentry sings in character as a young girl whose sick mother encourages her to become a prostitute: "Just be nice to the gentlemen, Fancy, and they'll be nice to you." If listeners expected a bleakly gothic tale of a wrecked Southern life, they got an anthem of empowerment, a story that Gentry would later describe as "my strongest statement for women's lib." Fancy escapes poverty to become the consort of powerful men, eventually becoming wealthy and powerful herself: "I charmed a king, a congressman, and an occasional aristocrat, and I got me a Georgia mansion and an elegant New York townhouse flat. And I ain't done bad."

Released in November 1969, "Fancy" proved to be a hit, even if it wasn't the game-changer Hall had predicted. It reached #26 on the *Billboard* country chart and #31 pop, her biggest solo hit since "Ode to Billie Joe." Gentry returned to Muscle Shoals in February and May 1970 to record songs for the album called *Fancy*, including covers of hits by Burt Bacharach, James Taylor, and Laura Nyro. The title track and the non-album single "Apartment 21" were the only original compositions she tracked at FAME.

But "Fancy" became a signature song for Gentry. She immediately incorporated it into her Vegas show, performing it in a red "satin dancin' dress" like the one worn by the character. Her sympathetic depiction of sex work makes it an outlier in country music, but the story has resonated with younger generations of fans and artists, and the song has been covered by Lynn Anderson, Reba McEntire, the alt-country act the Geraldine Fibbers, and many others. Gentry was careful to distance herself from the character in "Fancy," no matter that their lives traced a parallel arc from poverty to wealth. "I don't associate myself or my past with the song," she told the Memphis *Commercial Appeal* in December 1969. "I remember 'Billie Joe' very well. I tried to explain that the song was just a creation, but people just didn't believe me. They don't believe me about this one either."

"Fancy" was a pivotal record for everyone involved. In the late 1960s, Capitol Records was looking for fresher voices beyond their own in-house recording crews, in a bid to stay competitive with other majors and to better promote the regional labels it distributed. Gentry's new single was the first time Capitol hired

Artwork for Bobbie Gentry's 1970 album, *Fancy*

an outside producer to work with one of its own acts and therefore the first demonstration of how this program might allow artists more freedom. "Fancy" also served as a billboard advertising Muscle Shoals to the world. Its success corresponded with increased attention directed toward this unlikely recording hotbed, and every new article mentioned Gentry alongside Aretha Franklin and Wilson Pickett.

The Shoals—and FAME in particular—suddenly emerged as a place where careers might be revived and fortunes reversed. Little Richard recorded his emphatically funky comeback single there, 1970's "Freedom Blues"; the Osmonds recorded their 1971 #1 pop hit "One Bad Apple," which allowed them to compete with the Jacksons; and three years later none other than Paul Anka earned his first #1 in fifteen years with "(You're) Having My Baby," produced by Hall at FAME. Recorded over at Muscle Shoals Sound Studio, Cher's 1969 album *3614 Jackson Highway*, named for the studio's address, might not have sold well, but it did manage to establish her as a solo artist apart from husband Sonny Bono.

Those sessions were the last time Gentry would record so close to home. She cut *Patchwork* (1971) back in Los Angeles, and it turned out to be her final album. (A collection of holiday songs and another record with Campbell were recorded but not released.) She spent the 1970s in Vegas and retired from music and public life altogether in 1981. Her whereabouts are as mysterious as whatever Billie Joe threw off the Choctaw Bridge, but like Fancy, music got her where she needed to be. She ain't done bad.

Bobbie Gentry plays her Martin 5-18 guitar, which she held on the cover of her 1967 debut album, *Ode to Billie Joe.* PHOTO COURTESY OF FAME RECORDING STUDIO

SOUND & ACTION: MAKING HISTORY WITH

millie jackson

(AND THE SWAMPERS)

BY ERICKA BLOUNT

No one has mastered the art of unapologetic truth telling better than Millie Jackson. At eighty-one years old, she's still at it. Right now she's in a fight with her bank—it seems a scammer has taken a large sum of her money, but the bank officials promise it will be returned in forty-seven days.

Millie Jackson is, as she should be, cursing up a storm.

"In forty-seven days, I will have my money back. You won't have to call me to find out, 'cause I'll be in jail. Just turn on the news," she jokes during a phone call.

Jackson is a cacophony of sounds and actions, and her voice is still strong. Soon she's talking about Alabama's Muscle Shoals Sound Studio with reverence—the place where she cut her 1974 breakthrough album *Caught Up*, the 1975 sequel *Still Caught Up*, along with 1977's *Feeling Bitchy*, which (like *Caught Up*) went gold, and 1983's *E.S.P. (Extra Sexual Persuasion)*, all made with the Swampers band.

"Muscle Shoals was a big deal not because the musicians were white playing behind R&B artists. They were a big deal because they gave you the music you wanted," she says about the diverse

LP cover for Millie Jackson's 1977 album, *Feelin' Bitchy.*

This Fender Thinline Telecaster was played by Jimmy Johnson, a member of the Swampers and the Muscle Shoals Rhythm Section.

ARTIFACT COURTESY OF THE ALABAMA MUSIC HALL OF FAME

acts that came to Muscle Shoals, including Aretha Franklin, Etta James, Jimmy Cliff, and Bob Seger, to record with the Swampers—the core unit that featured bassist David Hood, drummer Roger Hawkins, keyboardist Bary Beckett, and guitarist Jimmy Johnson. "The musicians played country, R&B, gospel—whatever the hell you wanted them to be," she says.

Caught Up was her brainchild, a groundbreaking concept album recorded at Muscle Shoals Sound and Criteria studios. The album tracks the progress of a woman's affair with a married man: the A-side presented the mistress's point of view, and the B-side offered the wife's side of the story.

Jackson's first hit on *Caught Up* was a lush build-out of the Luther Ingram hit "(If Loving You is Wrong) I Don't Want to be Right." Ingram had recorded the song with the Swampers in 1972, two years earlier. Jackson turned it into a three-part, nine-minute suite where she sings, gives a half-confession, half-sermon, raps about the freedom, *and* bares the conflicts and loneliness of being a mistress—every line and squeal in lockstep with the studio musicians and a clock ticking in time. The band rises and falls with her until finally she explodes.

Controversy was born with the second cut, "The Rap," where she raps that when you're the mistress, "You don't have to wash nobody's funky drawers but your own." Apparently "funky drawers" was considered vulgar at the time, and audiences picketed famed DJ Frankie Crocker at radio station WBLS radio in New York. WJLD, a Black-oriented station in Birmingham,

Millie Jackson at the Hammersmith Odeon, London, England, 1978. PHOTO BY DAVID REDFERN

Alabama, triggered a similar backlash when they aired Jackson's full album cuts rather than censored radio edits. Both protests increased her visibility and record sales.

Jackson was expressing in songs what women said to each other—little of which was considered ladylike in the 1970s. *Caught Up* was a big deal for her and for the industry: presenting a Black woman artist who produced and managed herself, and who devised a bold album structure where one song ran into the next while she flowed from singing to rapping. Not just innovative, this was transformative.

While nowadays Jackson leads a relatively normal life in Atlanta, Georgia, she still holds enough fiery fever to slam down on the pedal of her 2017 Cadillac as she drives around listening to the country music station on her car radio. But then, she's still just enough of a small-town Southern girl to bump the car to just two practical places: "I drive to the post office and the grocery store," she says with a raspy cackle. "Case closed."

She takes umbrage at being referred to most often as a blues singer, when, she explains, she sings more country music than anything else. "When I started, if you were Black, you were singing the blues," she says. "Why y'all insist on calling me a blues singer when I only made one blues song in my life? And that was as a joke," she says.

She lists the parts that compose a country artist and notes that race has nothing to do with it: guitars, a good musician, subject matter that people can relate to, and good stories are what matters, she says. Growing up, "the country singers were singing about the blues and the blues singers were complaining about the blues. I liked the country singers because they always had things that you could relate to with what was going on in the world."

Born Mildred Virginia Jackson in Thomson, near Augusta, Georgia, in 1944, she grew up marked by country music and country culture every step of the way. Her father, Ty Rufus Jackson, raised her after her mother died in a freak fire accident when she was a toddler. He worked as a sharecropper and insisted on raising Millie on his own.

By age seven, she was rigging her radio to listen to Nashville stations; by ten, her father was making corn liquor, and Millie was serving glasses for one dollar at the house. Their home was where folks came to hear music, dance, and get drunk until Sunday morning when they would wake up and go to church. "We would order the special of the week, and we would have the music going and the men got the horse in the stable on Friday nights," she says with a wicked laugh.

Even though her grandfather was a minister, she doesn't think of herself as church folk. "I didn't come from the church, I was thrown into it. They thought I wasn't gonna live to be twenty-one." By her fifteenth birthday she was on a bus to Newark, New Jersey, where she worked as a model, waitress, and in the garment district before getting discovered on a five-dollar dare that she could sing better than the act on stage at a Harlem cafe.

Advertisement for Millie Jackson's single "Breakaway" and album of the same name, 1973.

OPPOSITE PAGE, TOP: Millie Jackson was known for her innovative spoken-word style, first demonstrated on her 1974 album *Caught Up*. PHOTO BY ANTHONY BARBOZA

BOTTOM: LP cover for Millie Jackson's 1974 concept album, *Caught Up*, Recorded at Muscle Shoals Sound Studio, it includes the single "(If Loving You Is Wrong) I Don't Want to Be Right."

Jackson went on the road as an opening act for Sam Cooke's brother L. C. Cooke and mastered genres from R&B to country and rock. Famous today for talking profusely (and profanely) to her live audience, she can no longer remember if it came about because she was nervous or forgot the words to the songs. "I would tell them: 'You spent your money with me. Kiss my ass, I say what I want to say.'"

Even though much of her music wasn't radio-friendly, that didn't keep her recordings out of bars, 8-tracks, and clubs. "She was a staple in those environments, that's where I heard her," remembered Dyana Williams, celebrated broadcaster and founder of Black Music Month. "She created a genre unto herself.

"She's considered one of the first female rappers. She's a playwright and a trendsetter," Williams continued. "She was probably one of the first Black women artists to get her own adio show [in Dallas at KKDA]."

Much of it traces back to her time with the Swampers. "At Muscle Shoals, they created the sound of R&B. They were all great musicians. They'd sing a line and somebody in the band played it off the top of their head," Millie recalls. "All the big record companies respected Muscle Shoals because if you were Black you needed to go to Muscle Shoals and let mother****ers know what you doing." Jackson says she related to and loved the laid-back vibe in the studio. "They acted a fool," she says with a big laugh. "But they could play, boy, they could play."

HOLY
TRINITY

THUNDERCLAP OVER sheffield

BY MARLIN GREENE

Leon Russell came to Muscle Shoals Sound Studio in the early '70s, where I was working back then, to record his *Carney* album. My admiration and respect for Leon's talent was amplified watching him work in the studio.

One summer day we were blessed with a good Alabama thunderstorm. The lightning was so bad it kept kicking the electric service off in the studio and shutting down our recording session. Leon sent the musicians out for a lunch break, and that left just the two of us in the studio. Leon suggested we record some of the storm.

Always anxious to experiment with different recording techniques, I selected a couple of good condenser mics and put one by the front door and one at the side door of the studio. I opened both doors so we could pick up the sounds from

Leon Russell at Muscle Shoals Sound Studio, early 1970s. PHOTO COURTESY OF MUSCLE SHOALS SOUND STUDIO

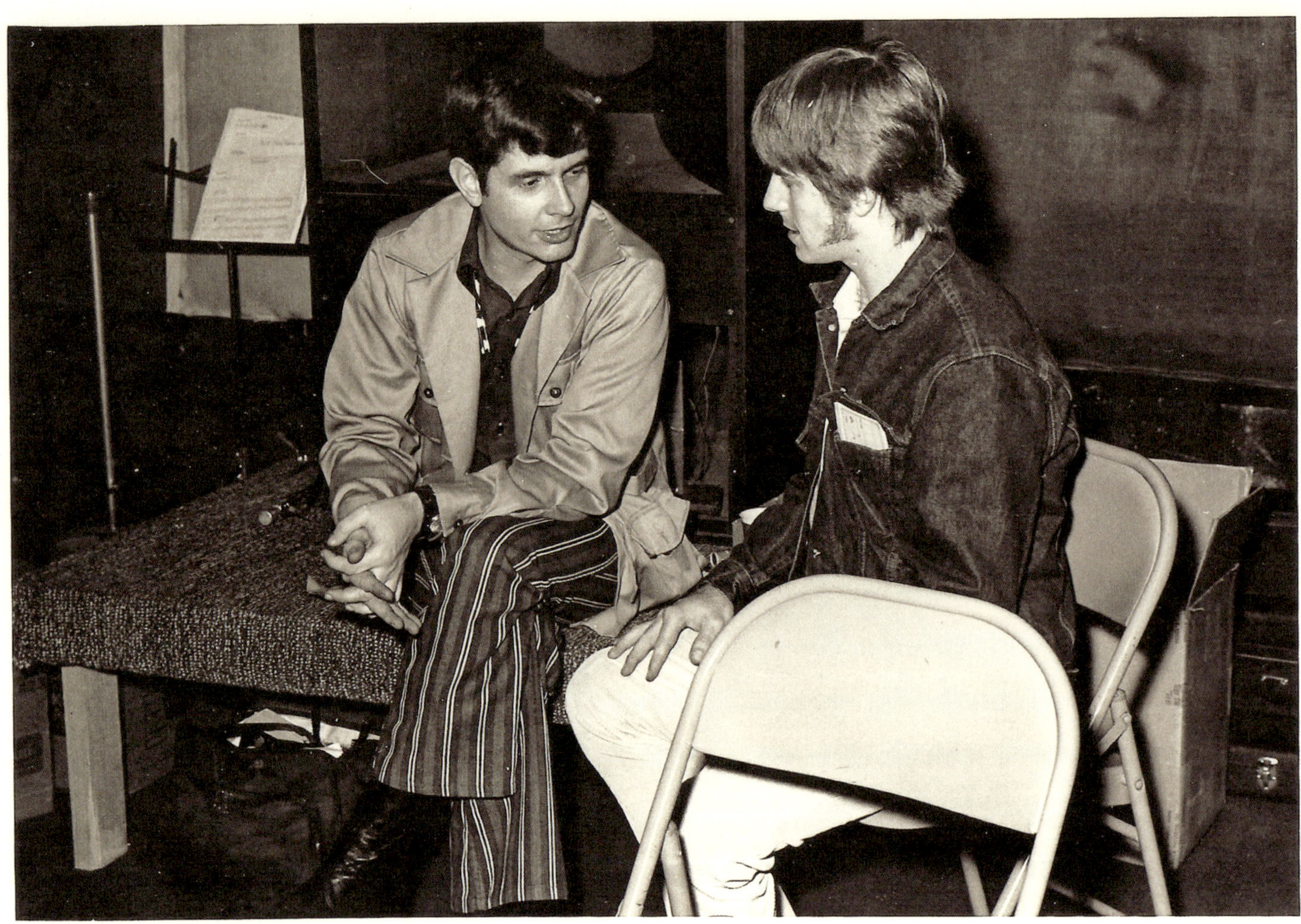

BOVE: Marlin Greene and Eddie Hinton in the studio, early 970s. A prolific songwriter and ace guitarist, Hinton layed on hit records by Wilson Pickett, the Staple ingers, Boz Scaggs, and others. His 1978 solo album, *ery Extremely Dangerous*, demonstrated his versatility s a writer, producer. and singer.

PPOSITE PAGE: The recording console at Muscle Shoals ound Studio's original location, 3614 Jackson Highway, arly 1970s.

HOTO COURTESY OF MUSCLE SHOALS SOUND STUDIO

outside. We could hear the traffic passing by, splashing the rain on the highway, and the rainwater—which was really coming down—rolling off the roof and beating on the stairs at the side door. Every few minutes there was a loud thunderclap accompanying the lightning.

Leon sat at the grand piano out in the studio with a note pad and started writing some lyrics to accompany the musical phrases he was tinkering with. After about ten minutes, Leon called up to

me in the control room, "OK Marlin, turn on the recorder." Immediately he was playing and singing a complete song he had just composed in the last few minutes.

The storm was still raging outside and the mics I had placed were producing an interesting mix of rain splashing, cars passing, and the occasional thunderclap as a background for Leon's performance. The lyrics—by the way—were about a guy sitting in a broken-down van on the highway in the rain. The song had a couple of verses, then a musical vamp of a few bars where Leon intended to play something catchy on the piano. I hit the record button and the tape was rolling. Leon's instant songwriting ability was now being demonstrated. He sang the two verses and started playing the piano vamp. About five seconds in, a huge thunderclap rolled through the Muscle Shoals area, and the control room speakers reproduced the low rumble.

The timing was perfect—right in the exact space to work with what Leon was playing. He looked up at me, never missing a beat, and just grinned. You can hear the recording of the song, just as it happened first time through, on Leon's *Carney* album, released in June 1972. It's called "Manhattan Island Serenade."

This episode confirmed for me that Leon deserved the title attributed to him by fans: "Master of Time and Space."

This piece first appeared on Marlin Greene's blog, Marlin's Substack.

A CERTAIN SONORITY

BY RJ SMITH

She was unknown to most of the musicians gathered at FAME in January 1967, the singer from Detroit that Atlantic Records producer Jerry Wexler had brought to town. The idea was to cut a whole album here, and the fuss Wexler was making about the session was itself unusual. He was convinced he could break her into the pop mainstream, though she had been trying just that for years while on Columbia Records with little success.

Songwriter Dan Penn knew the voice. As a boy in Vernon, Alabama, he had listened to WLAC late at night, heard her father, Reverend C. L. Franklin, deliver powerful sermons over the air and heard daughter Aretha sing gospel. "I loved all of that," Penn said. As her session approached, "I knew that she could sing, though she hadn't found the bull's-eye. . . . "
A clarifying storm was coming through.

Aspects of this Muscle Shoals story are disputed. But Wexler has said that he loved the band that Hall had put together, and also that he told Hall to hire a Black horn section. "I was a little anxious about presenting Aretha . . . with a wall-to-wall white band," he wrote in his autobiography, adding, "I also wanted a certain sonority that the brothers would bring to the horn section." For whatever reason, upon arrival the horn players were white, too, and that set up an unfortunate dynamic.

Aretha Franklin at the piano in Atlantic Studios, New York, January 1969. After her ill-fated session at FAME in 1967, Muscle Shoals musicians, including David Hood, Barry Beckett, Jimmy Johnson, and Roger Hawkins, traveled to New York to record with Franklin. PHOTO COURTESY OF MARK BECKETT

Apollo

Wexler, Penn, and others were all hanging around FAME on the day the quiet, unreadable Franklin and husband and manager Ted White entered the room. As the couple meandered through the studio, as quiet as it got, that was how much Penn could tell something was going to happen.

"She definitely was blessed, you know what I mean? She just looked like, *today's the day*."

Franklin talked a bit with some of the musicians until the time for greetings had expired. "She sat down at the piano and hit this unknown chord"—Penn hummed a sound—"I don't know what that chord was. But every musician in the room RAN to their instruments. It was a calling chord, you know?"

Someone played the demo of the first song they were to cut, "I Never Loved a Man (The Way That I Love You)." The tune was half-formed. "It was a really junky demo, didn't have much groove to it. It wasn't sung very well" by the songwriter, said Penn. How in the world are they cutting *this*?

More silence descended, and Spooner Oldham leaned in with a Fender Rhodes stroll that remixed the still air. Guitarist Chips

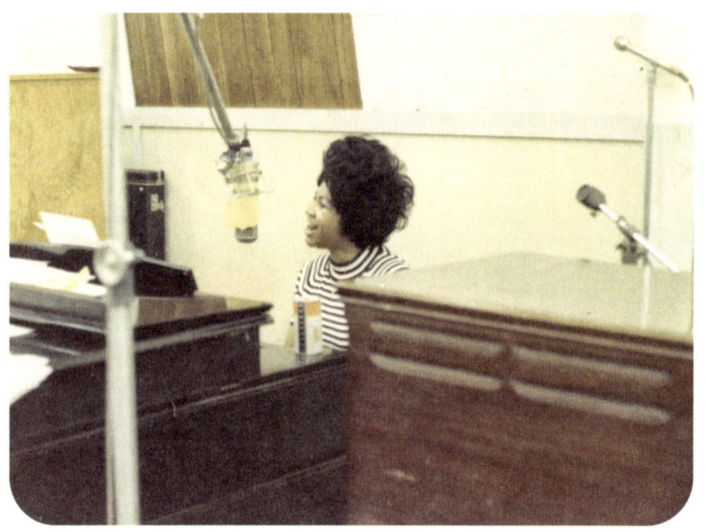

RIGHT, TOP AND BOTTOM: Muscle Shoals musician Spooner Oldham and Aretha Franklin at Atlantic Studios in New York, 1969. PHOTOS COURTESY OF MARK BECKETT

OPPOSITE PAGE: Aretha Franklin played this Apollo baby grand piano when she recorded her breakout pop and R&B hit, "I Never Loved a Man (The Way I Love You)," at FAME in 1967. The instrument was in use at the studio from 1961 to 1970. ARTIFACT COURTESY OF FAME RECORDING STUDIOS

Aretha Franklin with (from left) Atlantic Records producer Arif Mardin, session musicians Tommy Cogbill, Roger Hawkins, Jerry Jemmott, Spooner Oldham, Jimmy Johnson, and producer Tom Dowd, New York, 1968.

PHOTO COURTESY OF THE ESTATE OF DAVID GAHR/GETTY IMAGES

Atlantic Records producer Jerry Wexler poses with Aretha Franklin and her husband and manager, Ted White. MICHAEL OCHS ARCHIVE/GETTY IMAGES

Moman hollered, "Spooner's got it," and Franklin lightly stepped in behind FAME's baby grand piano. The song was cut quickly.

The musicians knew something special had happened. "There was much whooping, cheering, and slapping on the back," Oldham remembered later. "Everybody there knew it was a case of right place, right time for everyone involved and the Lord that day. There were tears in my eyes, in everyone's eyes."

Next, they turned to a song Moman and Penn had written, "Do Right Woman, Do Right Man." Wexler sent Penn to fine-tune the lyrics, as the band waited with Franklin and her husband. While waiting, a trumpet player shared a bottle with White.

Ten more songs to go for an album's worth of tracks. A rough instrumental track was recorded. But at some point the trumpet player and White were talking loosely, and then they were ranking on each other, and nothing good was going to happen as the bottle went back and forth while insults exchanged across racial lines. And then, Oldham said, "somebody pinched Aretha's butt." White pulled her out of the studio and took her to their hotel room.

It got worse there. Hall took it upon himself to be a peacemaker, and at 5 a.m. he hadn't come home yet. Linda Hall, Rick's wife, phoned Wexler at the hotel asking if he knew where Rick was. "Yeah, he's laying over here across my bed asleep," Wexler said, and he kept repeating "everything's fine now," in a way that made clear nothing was.

"He said, 'Well, there was a little altercation, but everything's okay.'"

Upon reflection, Wexler would later describe the little altercation between White and Hall as "*Walpurgisnacht* . . . things flying to pieces, everything going nuts."

Rick had gone over to patch things up. "He thought he could," said Linda. "But the bad thing was he got him a bottle of vodka before he went, and he was not a nice person when he was drinking. And so he went over there," intending to talk to White, "and they just had words and I think had blows."

Hall shouted, "Are you calling me a redneck?" at White, who answered, "Well, you sure look like one to me." Then Hall answered with a shove. White's response was a fist to Hall's jaw, and it continued from there, as the two rolled on the hotel room floor. Hall said he and White tried to throw each other off the hotel balcony.

Aretha Franklin's album *I Never Loved a Man (The Way That I Love You)* was certified gold by the RIAA (Recording Industry of America) in 1967, for sales of more than 500,000 units. ARTIFACT COURTESY OF FAME RECORDING STUDIOS

There was an obvious racial context to the confrontation: the kind of fragile harmony between the Black and white artists at Muscle Shoals could only survive if it was never probed too much. Consider this a moment of scrutiny. The need was to keep real world events outside the studio. It was easy enough to do, believed Penn. Asked about the struggle to integrate Alabama, he explained he wasn't paying attention. "My little part of the country where I came from was completely white. There was a few Black folks, but nothing to speak of. To tell you the truth it just didn't come up on my radar screen. I was deep into songwriting and deep into the studio. And I'd see the marches on TV and stuff like that and wonder, What's that all about? And it wasn't any, it just didn't come up. . . . I had stuff on my mind, and so I didn't pay much attention to it. It was—*odd*, I thought."

But the world was breaking through the front door of FAME. Not long after the sun came up, White and Franklin were flying back to New York, and Wexler told Hall, "I will bury you." Their world-changing relationship would rapidly wind down.

Ten days later, Wexler flew the FAME band to New York to make the Muscle Shoals record with Franklin that he believed would make her a star. In New York, the band cut her version of Otis Redding's "Respect," which was widely embraced as an anthem of emerging Black Power. Soul music's Black artists and audience wanted to put decision-making power in Black hands, and put the profit from Black artistry in Black hands as well.

Harrison Calloway was a Black trumpeter who found steady work in the Shoals starting at the end of the 1960s. His perspective was naturally a little different from Penn's. "I liked the fact that white people were getting involved with music I was raised on," Calloway said. "The thing I *didn't* like was that the opportunities for Black musicians seemed lessened. There was a tendency for us to say, 'These guys have their own thing, why can't we have *ours*?'"

That question would be explored in the rest of the 1970s. It is still being explored.

This bubblegum machine was at FAME throughout the 1960s and 1970s. Rick Hall's son Rodney Hall, the studio's current co-owner, commented half-jokingly that there "are probably still some of Otis Redding's pennies in there."

ARTIFACT COURTESY OF FAME RECORDING STUDIOS

OPPOSITE PAGE: Guitarist Jimmy Johnson and Otis Redding recording at FAME, 1966.

PHOTO COURTESY OF FAME RECORDING STUDIOS

MIGHTY SAM

It was the second storm in about a year, and it clarified more things. A tornado raked the southern edge of Muscle Shoals on April 4, 1968. Trees and powerlines came down, several buildings took a hit. Meanwhile, in a small studio at 3614 Jackson Highway in Sheffield, the band was setting up for a session.

Mighty Sam McClain had also blown into town. He was a gospel-soaked baritone, and the place he was setting up in was called Bevis Recording Studio, though that name was soon to be one of the things that would require clarification. In the spring of 1968, the band, soon to be nicknamed the Swampers, were playing hooky from their usual gig as the house band at FAME and freelancing this afternoon, just a couple miles from where they usually worked.

McClain and the band could spot the storm clouds filling the sky over the cemetery across the street. People thought this building was a funeral parlor, though it was more of a convenient place to store caskets, at least until someone visualized making music here. The music they were making now was a version of a thirty-four-year-old country song that McClain was calling "I Just Came to Get My Baby (Out of Jail)."

CLOCKWISE, FROM TOP LEFT: Session musicians Junior Lowe, David Hood, Barry Beckett, Roger Hawkins, and Jimmy Johnson in front of FAME, late 1960s.

PHOTO COURTESY OF FAME RECORDING STUDIOS

FINAL **THE COMMERCIAL APPEAL** FINAL

129th YEAR—No. 96 ••••• MEMPHIS, TENN., FRIDAY MORNING, APRIL 5, 1968 60 PAGES PRICE 10 CENTS

DR. KING IS SLAIN BY SNIPER

Looting, Arson Touched Off By Death

GUARDSMEN RETURN: CURFEW IS ORDERED

By RICHARD LENTZ

Looting, arson and shooting began minutes after the death of Dr. Martin Luther King Jr. lates last night and in hours Tennessee National Guardsmen arrived to take over street patrols in riot-torn Memphis.

Negroes began swarming into streets, smashing windows and setting fires shortly after the announcement of the civil rights leader's death at 7 p.m.

As the news of Dr. King's slaying flashed, Negroes clashed with police as far away as Miami, in Jackson, Miss., and in Nashville, where another 4,000 guardsmen were called out to keep the peace.

In Memphis, police had arrested 80 persons, including two juveniles and two women by 1 a.m. There were at least 21 persons reported hurt and a steady flow of injured was being treated at hospitals.

No one had been reported killed in the turmoil.

The most seriously injured person was Ellis Tate of 86 West Utah, whom police said was shot while looting. He was in critical condition at John Gaston Hospital.

Officers said he fired at officers with a rifle when they came into a liquor store he was looting. They returned his fire and he was hit.

A 24-hour general curfew was ordered last night, with travel allowed only for emergency or health reasons. Schools, shops and businesses were ordered closed. The curfew will remain in effect indefinitely.

At the biggest fire of the night, policemen armed with submachine guns and riot guns guarded firemen who were battling flames that arched 100 feet into the air at O. W. Ferrell Co. at 1001 North Second Street.

Within minutes, 14 pieces of fire equipment were on the scene. There were no incidents.

Firemen Battle Blaze At Ferrell Lumber Co. At 1001 North Second

An Editorial—

Memphis Needs Calm

Intensive Manhunt Is Quickly Mounted

President Johnson's Plane Is Reported En Route To Memphis; State Guard Alerted

By JOHN MEANS

A sniper shot and killed Dr. Martin Luther King last night as he stood on the balcony of a downtown hotel.

The most intensive manhunt in the city's history was touched off minutes after the shooting.

Violence broke out in Memphis, Nashville, Birmingham, Miami, Raleigh, Washington, New York and other cities as news of the assassination swept the nation.

National leaders, including President Lyndon Johnson, and aides close to the slain 39-year-old Nobel Peace Prize winner, urged the nation to stand calm and avoid violence.

The entire nation was tense.

It was learned early this morning that Air Force One — the President's plane — had left Washington. It may be en route to Memphis.

There was no confirmation that the President was aboard.

The slaying of Dr. King brought Tennessee National Guardsmen back into Memphis. The entire 11,000 men in the state guard were on alert early today.

Memphis was placed under a tight, 24-hour curfew by Mayor Henry Loeb.

All schools will be closed today. Parents were urged to keep their children at home.

A rifle bullet slammed into Dr. King's jaw and neck at 6:01 p.m.

He died in the emergency room at St. Joseph Hospital at 7:05 p.m.

King, the foremost American civil rights leader, was alone on the second-floor walk of the Lorraine Hotel at 406 Mulberry when the bullet struck.

Written and first recorded as "I'm Here to Get My Baby Out of Jail" by *National Barn Dance* duo Karl & Harty in 1934, the song was recorded by the Blue Sky Boys in 1936, and it was their tender version that likely inspired the Everly Brothers' immortal 1958 cover. Those early versions used tight duet harmonies to narrate a tragic story happening to somebody else—they humbly tell about an old woman pleading for her child to be set free.

But Mighty Sam was singing like this was something closer than a shared memory, and his was no folksong—it became pure soul-country music, full of grief, desperate to declare that a great misdeed has taken place. The finished record is worth one's time (released as a single on the Amy label).

Another thing about this: it was made on the day Martin Luther King was killed in Memphis. When the news arrived at the studio, bassist David Hood said that they all decided to call off the session out of respect for King, and everyone went home. And when they reconvened, something felt different.

"I'll tell you what happened," guitarist Jimmy Johnson said later. "There was a change from that night, from that point on. The rhythm & blues acts stopped coming to work with us, after that night.

"I'd say within a period of what—a year or so after that? —we were cutting almost all pop acts: Paul Simon, Cat Stevens, Rod Stewart. Everything switched from rhythm & blues and all of a sudden Black acts quit coming to our studio."

That's how it felt to the studio musicians. It wasn't quite as abrupt a change as that, and Black acts would continue recording in the Shoals. But a moment was passing, and racial currents it was once possible to ignore were coming out into the open. For whites, the moment was an awakening.

To Spooner Oldham the shift played out slowly. "It was nothing you could write down or see on paper. It was just in the air. I was the last one to understand it. I wondered why it was, because I'm the same. I play the same, I think the same."

"Nothing changed but everything changed," said Oldham. "I don't know why."

LEFT: Front page of *The Commercial Appeal*, Memphis, Tennessee, April 5, 1968.

RIGHT: This Burly electric guitar was custom built by craftsman Jeff Ayers for Muscle Shoals session guitarist Travis Wammack. Wammack began his career at age twelve in Memphis. His passion for wrangling rattlesnakes earned him the nickname "Snake Man."

ARTIFACT COURTESY OF THE ALABAMA MUSIC HALL OF FAME

WAH! WAH! WAH! WAH!

Already by the spring of 1968, the FAME house band had been thinking of going out on their own. The Swampers had come up through Rick Hall's school of hard knocks and were tired of the knocks. Hall kept a tight grip on everyone who worked in the studio—even, it was said, making Clarence Carter, who was blind, punch his timeclock. Hall let people know when he wasn't happy with what they were playing, pointing out, say, that he had brought in more guitarists—you could see them, sitting next to Travis Wammack on the couch in the lobby—to do their job.

Hall was haunted by the prospect of failure, of being extinguished, and he felt that through a demonstration of his own work habits and his seriousness of purpose, hits would follow.

It was indisputably working in terms of hits: by 1968, the template established at Muscle Shoals had produced an outpouring of great records. Percy Sledge's success had convinced Jerry Wexler to send Wilson Pickett, Arthur Conley, Clarence Carter, Etta James, and Aretha Franklin to the Shoals. In a setting where there was little distraction outside the studio,

Junior Lowe, Clarence Carter, Roger Hawkins, Jimmy Johnson, and Rick Hall at FAME, late 1960s.

PHOTO COURTESY OF FAME RECORDING STUDIOS

This Rolodex from the desk of Rick Hall was used in the 1960s.

ARTIFACT COURTESY OF FAME RECORDING STUDIOS

OPPOSITE PAGE: Gene "Bowlegs" Miller, Billy Foster, Etta James, and Rick Hall at FAME, 1967.

MICHAEL OCHS ARCHIVE/GETTY IMAGES

Black singers and white players collaborated in tight formation on a creative and cultural level rare anywhere in the country.

When the first Muscle Shoals Rhythm Section left for Nashville in 1964, guitarist Jimmy Johnson saw opportunity. He already had a foot in the door at FAME. "And there we were. Rick Hall had no one else to get but us guys."

The Shoals had no musician's union local, and Hall worked the new players until he was satisfied. In Nashville, a recording session typically cut four songs in three hours for a standard unit of pay per hour. But early on, when the Shoals band and producer were both learning how to operate a studio, time was elastic.

"Rick Hall later on realized that early takes were usually the best takes. But during the period that we grew up with him learning to produce, we'd be on take ninety-eight about the third day in," recalled Johnson. "And back then he was paying us a session like every three songs. Now, it might take us a *week* to cut three songs. So, we got our practice in."

Future audiences would know them as the Swampers, but they weren't anybody yet in 1964. Hall had a strong, general idea of what was good, and he got his point across.

"We'd go in and play and he'd say 'No, that's terrible. No, you can't do this.' And he'd berate us," bassist David Hood remembered. "But we learned because we hated being bitched at so much. We would learn. You would have to."

Drummer Roger Hawkins knew the system. "He used to say, 'Even if I ask you to go out in the middle of the studio and play a paper bag, if that's what I want, then that's what you do.' He really gave me some wisdom about the recording studio and how players should aim to please the producer. The producer is always right; if he tells you to play on the snare side to get a crisper sound, you do it.

"Rick Hall had a habit of coming down hard on you at the wrong time. He'd do *subtle* things like hit the talkback button and say, 'Roger, your drums sound like s***.' That would embarrass me to high heaven. I would want to crawl under the drums rather than play them." They were recording mono, cutting the rhythm track live. If anyone hit a wrong note, everybody had to start over on a new take. It created community on the floor, and at times, resentment.

"I learned to just cancel my feelings and put everything out of my mind except the job at hand," Hood said. "I loved the job, I was learning new things and getting paid. Even though it wasn't a lot of money, it was better than working at the tire store."

Muscle Shoals session musician and Swampers drummer Roger Hawkins used this Slingerland snare drum with his first band, Spooner & the Spoons. The group, which included Spooner Oldham, Dan Penn, and Junior Lowe, recorded at FAME, c. 1965.

ARTIFACT COURTESY OF THE ALABAMA MUSIC HALL OF FAME

OPPOSITE PAGE: Rick Hall sits at the recording console at FAME, 1970s. Of the Wilson Pickett sessions, Hall said, "I stayed hunched over that console like a spider, determined not to miss a lick and get every slider on the console exactly right in order to get every ounce of energy into the record."

PHOTO COURTESY OF FAME RECORDING STUDIOS

Wilson Pickett and session musicians at FAME, c. 1966. FROM LEFT: Spooner Oldham, Junior Lowe, Pickett (seated), Roger Hawkins, and Jimmy Johnson.

PHOTO COURTESY OF FAME RECORDING STUDIOS

fame RECORDING STUDIOS
HOME OF (ORIGINAL)
Muscle Shoals Sound

Sticker for FAME, 1970s

ARTIFACT COURTESY OF THE ROCK & ROLL HALL OF FAME

They made many great records together. They made Wilson Pickett's "Mustang Sally" together, and that record is fire. It was late 1966, and Hall had booked a big one. Ever since Atlantic Records picked up Percy Sledge and his hit "When a Man Loves a Woman" at the beginning of the year, Atlantic's third eye Jerry Wexler had held FAME deep in his thoughts. He was sending hitmakers Hall's way, to see what might rub off when Black star power collided with unknown white studio cats.

Here's the rub: right at the end of the song's first verse, when Pickett is telling Mustang Sally, "You been running all over town now / I guess I'll have to put your flat feet on the ground," right then Spooner Oldham pounds out on his organ four echo-sodden on-the-off-beat squalls that roar like a Harley-Davidson hog revving in the Crystal Cave. It resets the whole song; it is unspeakably fun.

And when he talks about what he did on "Mustang Sally," Oldham first describes hearing the demo of the hard-groove

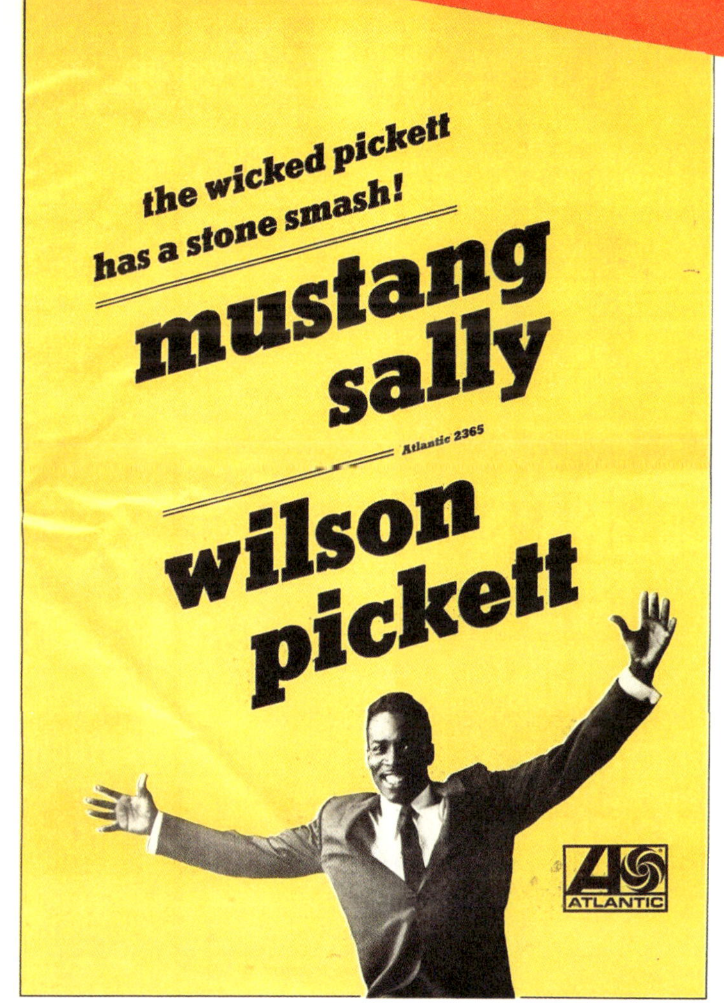

Billboard advertisement, November 19, 1966

COURTESY OF FAME RECORDING STUDIOS

Wilson Pickett, Spooner Oldham (piano), and Junior Lowe (guitar), at FAME, c. 1966. Jerry Wexler recalled that nobody could control Pickett in the studio, but “it didn’t matter, because the magic was in the music and the music was so deeply ingrained in Muscle Shoals—in guitarists like Eddie Hinton, keyboardists like Spooner Oldham, songwriters like Donnie Fritts.” PHOTO COURTESY OF FAME RECORDING STUDIOS

number. There was no keyboard on the prototype, no space for him, and Pickett had already gone around the room and told the other musicians things to play.

"I don't hear anything in there," Oldham thought to himself. "And it's time to start doing something, playing it. And I'm thinking, 'Well, I want my job. I want to work here, I want to be on this, but I don't have a part.' And so, I've got to create a part. What's it gonna be?

"I'm sitting there on the stool, the organ's on, and I'm just daydreaming a minute. 'I wonder what it would sound like if you rode a motorcycle through the studio?' And that's what I emulated, that sound on the organ." *Wah! Wah! Wah! Wah!* And as quick as he was playing it, Hall in the booth was catching on and amplifying the echo to match the moment.

These were people on both sides of the glass who had lived close to the bone, who had missed meals or known those who had.

Recorded at FAME and co-produced by Rick Hall and Jerry Wexler, Wilson Pickett's version of "Mustang Sally" was a pop and R&B hit in 1966.

THE MUSCLE SHOALS SOUND

In 1969, the Swampers left FAME and set up—with a loan from Jerry "I will bury you" Wexler—in the crackerbox on Jackson Highway. They were capable of playing all kinds of music, and they made much of their independence.

"It's not the room, it's the musicians" was their guiding philosophy and one that the situation demanded. Paul Simon was eager to visit after he heard what the Swampers had done backing the Staple Singers on "I'll Take You There" in 1972. According to keyboardist Barry Beckett, they shocked Simon by polishing off his "Take Me to the Mardi Gras" in a half hour after he came to town. So Simon pulled out other songs and asked which ones they wanted to record together next.

As they pondered, it was pouring rain outside; the studio had a leak over the sound board. Engineer Jerry Masters had taped sanitary napkins to the ceiling. Simon thought the whole setup was "esoteric"; together they proceeded to record "Kodachrome," "St. Judy's Comet," "One Man's Ceiling Is Another Man's Floor," and "Loves Me Like a Rock," key moments on 1973's *There Goes Rhymin' Simon.*

Greetings from Muscle Shoals Sound Studio, early 1970s.
FROM LEFT: Roger Hawkins, Barry Beckett, David Hood, Jimmy Johnson, Carol Little Buckins, Steve Melton, Diane Butler, Pierce Pettus, and Bobby Heathcote.
PHOTO COURTESY OF MUSCLE SHOALS SOUND STUDIO

ACKSON HIGHWAY

David Hood and Cher take a dirtbike ride on the front lawn of Muscle Shoals Sound Studio, 1969. PHOTO COURTESY OF MARK BECKETT

LEFT: Musician and producer Mickey Buckins wore this fringed buckskin jacket on the cover of the 1969 album *Solid Gold from Muscle Shoals, The Fame Gang*. ARTIFACT COURTESY OF MICKEY BUCKINS

It was the musicians. Bob Seger came and recorded "Night Moves," "Mainstreet," "Rock and Roll Never Forgets," and "Old Time Rock & Roll." That last one was written primarily by Muscle Shoals hitmaker George Jackson and fueled by a guitar solo played by a stranger pulled out of the parking lot that day. Everyone was in the groove. Rod Stewart came early one morning and thought the guy setting up was the cleaning man, when it was bassist David Hood. As the rest of the Swampers arrived, Stewart was baffled and asked Hood when the Black band he expected would arrive.

Folks beyond the music business paid attention. The music press noticed, depicting the Quad Cities as some spa set off

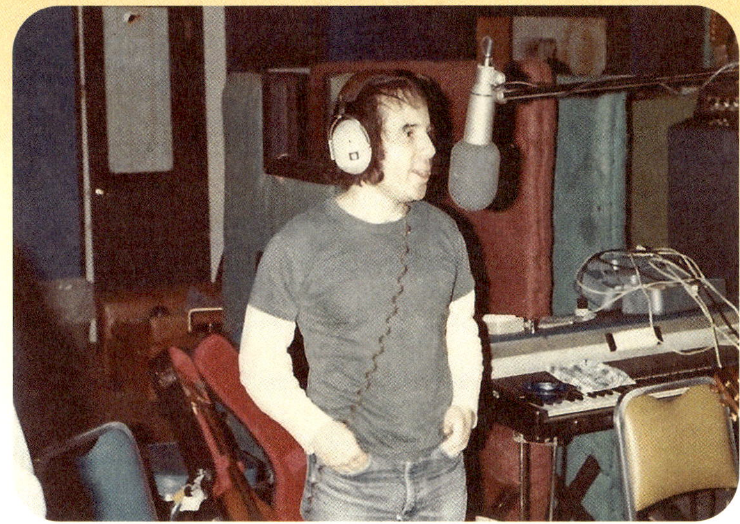

At Muscle Shoals Sound (CLOCKWISE FROM TOP LEFT): Paul Simon, Mavis Staples with Roger Hawkins, Bob Dylan (CENTER), and Charlie Watts of the Rolling Stones with Roger Hawkins.

in the steamy swamp maples, its tractor beam pulling rock and pop's biggest stars closer to the truth, to a healing simplicity that held funk and groove and "mistakes" in mystical congruence. There was Cher, and the Rolling Stones, Liza Minelli, Traffic, Jimmy Cliff in the Shoals. The roll call of pop stars was so consistent for a while that listeners might imagine them all hobnobbing by a barbeque stand.

The session guys were romanticized as dirt bike Buddhas who blurred genres. But when Willie Nelson came to town in 1973, another approach was essential. "Willie Nelson was the first [time when we] knew this was gonna be country," said Barry Beckett. Nelson drove in from Texas by himself, in what Hood calls "this dusty, dirty Mercedes Benz." He walked in carrying a guitar and his suitcase, which he threw down on the ground before saying,

"Let's cut." They were a flexible band, but there were limits. "We said, 'Wait, wait, wait,'" remembered Hood. "We've got to learn each song and do it like that." But Willie didn't want to do it like that—he wanted to go through the album song by song as he envisioned it, playing each one live and recording it.

"That would've been wonderful, but we had to learn the songs," Hood said. They were proud of not needing to prep, but Willie Nelson demanded a new level of openness to the moment. In the end they had the whole album, *Phases and Stages*, cut in two days. There were important contributions from country session masters, but the heart and soul of the sound is the Swampers, including guitarist Pete Carr.

Time will take care of itself so just leave time alone
Pick up the tempo just a little and take it on home
Willie Nelson, "Pick Up the Tempo"

Fairly viewing themselves as rhythm masters of time and space, they assumed their first country record called for a more rigid

Suit worn by Pops Staples and matching jumpsuits worn by Cleotha, Yvonne, and Mavis Staples of the Staple Singers in 1971.

GIFT OF MARTY STUART, WILLARD AND PAT WALKER CHARITABLE FOUNDATION, AND LORETTA AND JEFF CLARKE. FROM THE MARTY STUART COLLECTION

The Fame Gang (FROM TOP LEFT, CLOCKWISE): **Mickey Buckins, Ronnie Eades, Harrison Calloway, Junior Lowe, Jesse Boyce, Freeman Brown, and Aaron Varnell, c. 1970.**

PHOTO COURTESY OF FAME RECORDING STUDIOS

Jerry Wexler, in a top hat, and Willie Nelson outside Muscle Shoals Sound Studio, where Nelson recorded the Wexler-produced album, *Phases and Stages*, in 1973.

PHOTO COURTESY OF DICK COOPER

Session guitarist Pete Carr recording at Muscle Shoals Sound Studio, 1970s. Carr's unmistakable guitar tone can be heard on his solo on Bob Seger's "Mainstreet." PHOTO COURTESY OF MUSCLE SHOALS SOUND STUDIO

TOP RIGHT: David Hood's Muscle Shoals Sound Studio satin jacket, 1980s. ARTIFACT COURTESY OF DAVID HOOD

BOTTOM: Willie Nelson previewed *Phases and Stages*, at the Country Dinner Playhouse in Austin, March 18, 1974. GIFT OF THE ESTATE OF CHET FLIPPO

approach. That was before Nelson started playing Trigger, his worn and torn Martin classical guitar. "We thought, 'Gosh his timing is crazy.' We thought we had to be metronomes, and he was all over the place," said Hood. "If anything, he had to compromise [to] play with us."

In *Texas Monthly* magazine's epic ranking of all 154 of Willie Nelson's albums, they place *Phases and Stages* at #1, calling it "a perfect album."

FAME
RECORDING STUDIOS
PRODUCTIONS
PUBLISHING CO.

WE CAN DO IT FROM HERE

John Paul White was born in Tuscumbia, Alabama, in another time: the modern era. Born in 1972, he moved with his family to Loretto, Tennessee, about thirty miles from the Shoals, where he grew up on a chicken farm.

But one day when he was a kid, his parents were driving through Florence and his mom pointed at the FAME studio building from the car. "They record songs in there," she said. At the time, "I didn't even understand what that meant," says White. "Who?"

"And of all the people that she could have mentioned, she said, 'The Osmonds.'" Which was good, not just because "One Bad Apple" is, deal with it, a pretty great record, but also because if she had named Aretha Franklin he says he wouldn't have known yet who that was. "I was like, 'Oh, that's cool.'"

Slowly, unforcedly, traces of Shoals music entered his consciousness. His band began playing in the bars around the Alabama–Tennessee border, and those audiences were calling out for "Mustang Sally" and other staples.

"When I started playing those bars, David Hood would be there playing, or Spooner would be sitting in with somebody,

FAME Recording Studios on Avalon Avenue in Muscle Shoals as it looks today.
PHOTO COURTESY OF FAME RECORDING STUDIOS

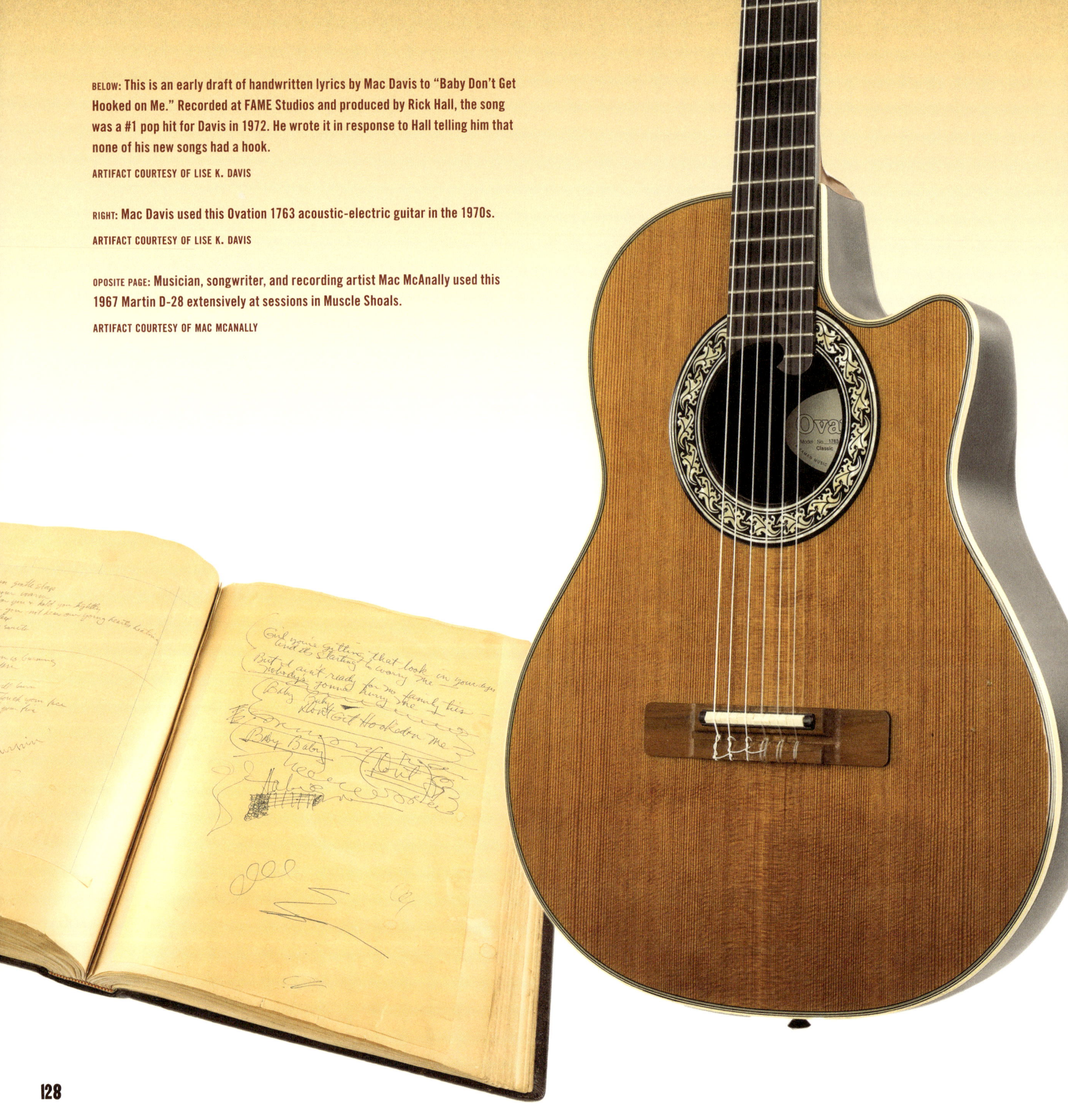

BELOW: This is an early draft of handwritten lyrics by Mac Davis to "Baby Don't Get Hooked on Me." Recorded at FAME Studios and produced by Rick Hall, the song was a #1 pop hit for Davis in 1972. He wrote it in response to Hall telling him that none of his new songs had a hook.

ARTIFACT COURTESY OF LISE K. DAVIS

RIGHT: Mac Davis used this Ovation 1763 acoustic-electric guitar in the 1970s.

ARTIFACT COURTESY OF LISE K. DAVIS

OPOSITE PAGE: Musician, songwriter, and recording artist Mac McAnally used this 1967 Martin D-28 extensively at sessions in Muscle Shoals.

ARTIFACT COURTESY OF MAC MCANALLY

Roger Clark, Roger Hawkins, they'd play," he says. Somebody would pull him aside and be like, "Do you know who that is?" "No," he would honestly tell them. But he would learn, and soon he came to understand the musical tradition of the Shoals.

He watched how they did it, noted what got audiences in his time moving and what got them listening. And today, he says, "I wouldn't take anything for that education.

"But I knew it wasn't the music I was going to make. I never ever set out to do anything someone else had done. I don't think I consciously thought about it, but that just bored me." Learning how to make music that didn't come so easily, he says, "probably slowed my career down quite a bit." But he also knew what he had in his back pocket. "The full support of David and Jimmy and Roger and those guys [saying], 'We're cheering for you, man. Come play this gig with us. You need to meet this dude. . . . '"

The hungry days were back, for some, and for many the landscape was being reshaped. The pop star money dried up in the 1980s. At FAME, Rick Hall had survived and thrived after the Swampers left, but by the 1980s he was increasingly focused on a stable of songwriters—many of whom were writing country hits—and on lucrative music publishing.

Newer studios took root: there was Cypress Moon, in a former naval facility on a bluff over the river, and Wishbone, a hotbed of 1980s country where Alabama, Shenandoah, and

Hank Williams Jr. all did important work. Music Mill was a studio and a publishing house where, co-owner Al Cartee once explained in *Billboard*, “my idea was to put country artists and country songs with pop musicians.” It worked, and Narvel Felts, Roy Clark, Waylon Jennings, Bobby Bare, Carl Perkins, and many more all recorded there.

The Shoals was a songwriting and country hotbed in this period. But today White notes, there’s a lively scene built around bands, rather than powerhouse studios. The late 1980s and into the 1990s were a rough time for working bands in the Shoals. That’s precisely when he moved back.

“The Drive-By Truckers were famously leaving to go to Athens because there was just nothing going on here,” he recalls. “People were holding on so tightly to the past. They didn’t care about the present or the future. It was just legacy and what gets tourists here. And it never dawned on anybody to support local musicians and help them out and keep it going.

“The whole place became a museum, and I understood them leaving.” He distances himself from the sounds of his predecessors, it could be said, the way the Shoals session masters once pushed away from country music—to make something original right there, at home. To belong.

He formed the Civil Wars with Joy Williams in 2008; they won a Grammy in 2012. Along with musician Ben Tanner and Will Trapp he formed Single Lock Records. The first albums he

TOP: The Osmonds autographed this photo for Rick Hall’s sons, 1970. PHOTO COURTESY OF FAME RECORDING STUDIOS

ABOVE: Hank Williams Jr., Rick Hall, and Waylon Jennings working on Williams’s 1977 album, *The New South*. PHOTO COURTESY OF FAME RECORDING STUDIOS

OPPOSITE PAGE: Jason Isbell used this First Act Custom Delgada LS electric guitar with the Drive-By-Truckers and the 400 Unit. ARTIFACT COURTESY OF JASON ISBELL

John Paul White co-owns Single Lock Records, based in Florence.
ARTIFACT COURTESY OF JOHN PAUL WHITE

produced in his life were the last two records made by Donnie Fritts, a songwriter and musician who was there from the very beginning of the scene. *June: A Tribute to Arthur Alexander*, came out in 2018; Fritts died a year later.

White cites the regional presence of Jason Isbell, Brittany Howard, the Secret Sisters, Gary Nichols, and others as a sign of the existence of a lively contemporary Shoals scene. Building and bending tradition. "We all kind of figured out that we love

This 1957 Fender Telecaster belonged to Muscle Shoals session guitarist, producer, and recording engineer Pete Carr. The instrument was also used by Duane Allman when he and Carr were members of Hour Glass. ARTIFACT COURTESY OF BRIAN McGEE

our ancestry. We have stood on their shoulders and they have been very supportive and generous to us. But it wasn't doing us a damn bit of good, and we had to make our own hay."

The musicians of his time have come to draw the same conclusion that Rick Hall arrived at when he was sleeping in his car and holding court at Spar studio, above the City Drug Store long ago.

"I don't think we consciously said it, but we all decided the same thing: We can do it from here. We don't have to go to them. If it's good enough, they'll come to us."

The doorway at present-day FAME Recording Studios

20 GREAT RECORDS FROM MUSCLE SHOALS

BY ROB BOWMAN

Here are just a few interesting highlights among the many outstanding recordings made in Muscle Shoals, presented in chronological order. Anyone who has listened to the music made in Muscle Shoals could easily put together an entirely different list.

BELOW: Gold record plaque for "Land of 1000 Dances" by Wilson Pickett presented to FAME Studios in recognition of one million records sold.

ARTIFACT COURTESY OF THE ALABAMA MUSIC HALL OF FAME

ARTHUR ALEXANDER
"YOU BETTER MOVE ON"

Dot 16309—1961
Writer: Arthur Alexander

Local bellhop Arthur Alexander wrote "You Better Move On," and Rick Hall produced the song at his first studio, a converted tobacco warehouse. Hall leased the single to Dot Records. "You Better Move On" reached #24 on the pop charts. Two years later the Rolling Stones covered the song for their self-titled British EP. Rick Hall used the production royalties from the single to purchase the lot for a new studio in Muscle Shoals.

JIMMY HUGHES
"STEAL AWAY"

FAME 6401—1964
Writer: Jimmy Hughes

"Steal Away" was the first song that Jimmy Hughes had ever written, and it was the first recording at Rick Hall's new FAME studio at 603 East Avalon Avenue. Hall released "Steal Away" on his own FAME label in May 1964. Later, Vee-Jay Records released the record nationally. It reached #17 on the *Billboard* Hot 100 charts.

BOBBY MOORE & THE RHYTHM ACES
"SEARCHING FOR MY LOVE"

Checker 1129—1965
Writer: Bobby Moore

In the fall of 1965, tenor saxophonist Bobby Moore and his group rented studio time at FAME. Jimmy Johnson, who engineered the recording, remembered, "They came in and I think they only had $50, and studio time was $17.50 an hour. I cut the record in less than two hours." "Searching for My Love" peaked at #7 R&B while also entering the pop Top Thirty. In 2021, Robert Plant and Alison Krauss covered the song for their album *Raise the Roof.*

PERCY SLEDGE
"WHEN A MAN LOVES A WOMAN"

Atlantic 2326—1966
Writers: Calvin Lewis and Andrew Wright

Percy Sledge was a hospital orderly who also sang on weekends. After being turned down by Rick Hall, Sledge auditioned for studio owner Quin Ivy, who was struck by Sledge's voice and the rudiments of a song he had. However, the song lacked coherent lyrics and a bridge. Marlin Greene added the bridge, and he and Ivy rewrote the lyrics, giving the song a new title. "When a Man Loves a Woman" would become the best-selling single in Atlantic's history, peaking at the top of both the R&B and the pop charts.

ARTHUR CONLEY "SWEET SOUL MUSIC"

Atco 6463—1967
Writers: Sam Cooke, Otis Redding, Arthur Conley

In January 1967, Otis Redding brought Arthur Conley to FAME. Conley suggested they cut Sam Cooke's "Yeah Man." Redding liked the idea but decided the song would benefit from a lyric rewrite. With all new lyrics, Redding copped the melody of "Yeah Man" and adapted a musical theme from the movie *The Magnificent Seven* and turned it into an opening horn-section hook. The single stormed to #2 on both the R&B and pop charts.

CLARENCE CARTER "SLIP AWAY"

Atlantic 2508—1968
Writers: William Armstrong, Wilbur Terrell, Marcus Daniel

"Slip Away" was recorded in mid-1967 but stayed in the can until it was released as the B-side of Clarence Carter's April 1968 release "Funky Fever." Carter later said, "I think it was the lyric and the subtle arrangement that really made it attractive to people. I played the guitar and did something on it that I'd always wanted to do." "Slip Away" soared to #2 R&B while crossing over to #6 pop.

R. B. GREAVES "TAKE A LETTER MARIA"

Atco 6714—1969
Writer: R. B. Greaves

The Swampers—Rick Hall's former session musicians—held the first sessions at their Muscle Shoals Sound Studio in April 1969. By the time R. B. Greaves arrived at the studio in August, they had yet to record a hit. When he showed up, Greaves started to play on an acoustic guitar the songs he planned to cut. It didn't take long for the rhythm section to work out an arrangement for "Take a Letter Maria." It peaked at #2 on the pop charts and #10 R&B in November 1969.

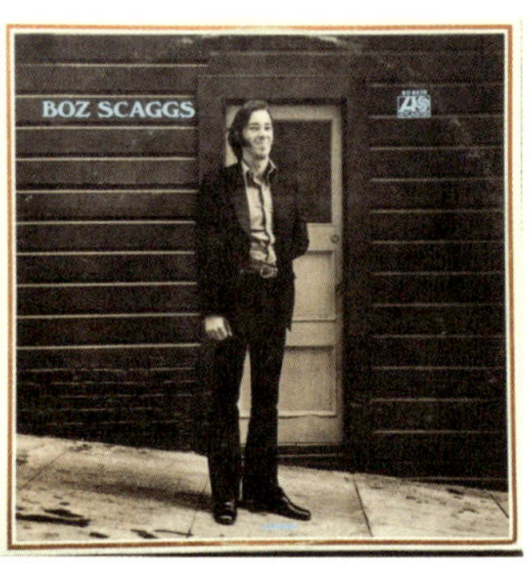

BOZ SCAGGS "LOAN ME A DIME"

Atlantic LP SD8239—1969
Writer: Fenton Robinson

Boz Scaggs was the third artist to record an album at the new Muscle Shoals Sound Studio. "Loan Me a Dime" was recorded with the Swampers for his self-titled album and clocks in at just over twelve minutes. The result was epic. Interweaving with Duane Allman's soaring lead guitar lines, Eddie Hinton added wonderful fills. The result, even though it wasn't heard by many at the time, was the most transcendent recording of Boz Scaggs's career.

BOBBIE GENTRY
"FANCY"

Capitol 2675—1969
Writer: Bobbie Gentry

In April 1969, Rick Hall signed an exclusive deal to produce artists for Capitol Records. At the same time, his rhythm section left to start their own studio. After quickly forming a new house band, the first artist he asked Capitol to work with was Bobbie Gentry. Hall suggested that she write another narrative song, like her 1967 hit "Ode to Billie Joe." The result was "Fancy," which went to #31 pop and #26 country. In 1991, Reba McEntire covered "Fancy," taking it to #8 on the country charts.

CANDI STATON
"STAND BY YOUR MAN"

FAME 1472—1970
Writers: Tammy Wynette and Billy Sherrill

Clarence Carter had brought former gospel singer Candi Staton to FAME in 1968. After four standout R&B singles, Rick Hall had Staton cover Tammy Wynette's #1 country hit "Stand by Your Man." Staton embraced the song, turning in an impassioned vocal, providing her with her biggest hit at FAME, peaking at #4 R&B while reaching #24 pop.

WILLIE HIGHTOWER
"WALK A MILE IN MY SHOES"

FAME 1465—1970
Writer: Joe South

In late 1969, Joe South had released "Walk a Mile in My Shoes," which became a #12 pop hit. Rick Hall decided to cover it with Willie Hightower, reasoning that he would get it on the R&B charts and might take away some of South's pop airplay and sales. The result was one of the greatest FAME singles, featuring an impassioned vocal from Hightower. Hitting #26 on the R&B charts, it was the most successful of the fourteen singles Hightower released.

ROLLING STONES
"WILD HORSES"

Rolling Stones Records RS-19101—1971
Writers: Mick Jagger and Keith Richards

While on tour in 1969, the Rolling Stones recorded for three days at Muscle Shoals Sound. On the third night, they tackled a country-flavored ballad called "Wild Horses." One of the hangers on at the session was Memphis musician Jim Dickinson, who began noodling on an old tack piano as the band started working out an arrangement. The Stones approved. That gutsy move got Dickinson a dream credit on a Rolling Stones record. Released as a single in 1971, "Wild Horses" reached #28 pop.

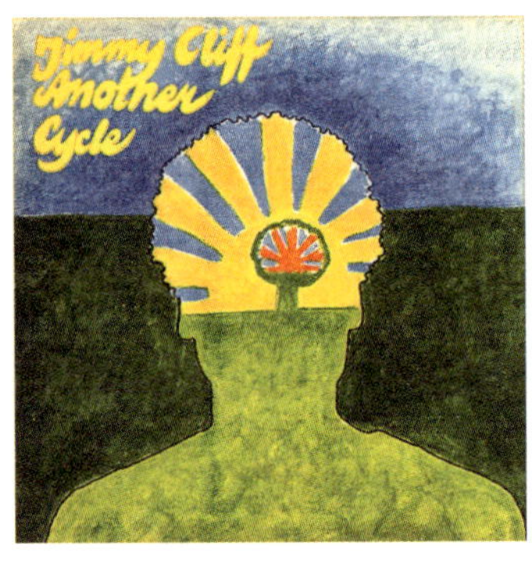

JIMMY CLIFF
"SITTING IN LIMBO"

Island LP ILPS 9159—1971
Writers: Jimmy Cliff and Guilly Bright

Jamaican artist Jimmy Cliff flew to Alabama with producers Guilly Bright and Chris Blackwell for sessions at Muscle Shoals Sound on April 25 and 26, 1970. Cliff had been releasing records in Jamaica and Great Britain since 1961, but he had yet to be heard by many in the U.S. Cliff returned in March 1971 to finish recording for the album *Another Cycle* (released June 1971), including "Sitting in Limbo," which was released as a single in the U.K. in August. Cliff would become an international star following the release of the Jamaican film *The Harder They Come* in 1972.

LEON RUSSELL
"TIGHT ROPE"

Shelter 7325—1972
Writer: Leon Russell

In August 1971, Leon Russell went to Muscle Shoals for his 1972 album, *Carney*. Marlin Greene engineered while Russell and Denny Cordell handled production. Over three days, Russell finished three songs: "Tight Rope," "Out in the Woods," and "Manhattan Island Serenade." The rest of the album was cut at Russell's own Skyhill Studio in Hollywood and Paradise Studios in Oklahoma. "Tight Rope" was released as a sin gle, reaching #11 on the *Billboard* charts.

THE STAPLE SINGERS
"I'LL TAKE YOU THERE"

Stax 0125—1972
Writer: Al Bell

The same week the Staple Singers cut "Respect Yourself" with the Muscle Shoals Rhythm Section, they also recorded their #1 R&B and pop single "I'll Take You There." The record's intro section, bass line, and general groove were lifted from a 1969 Jamaican instrumental recording by the Harry J. All Stars entitled "The Liquidator." "I'll Take You There" has only four lyric lines. The rest of the song consists of Mavis's ad lib vocal and the reggae groove and bass line refined by the Muscle Shoals Rhythm Section.

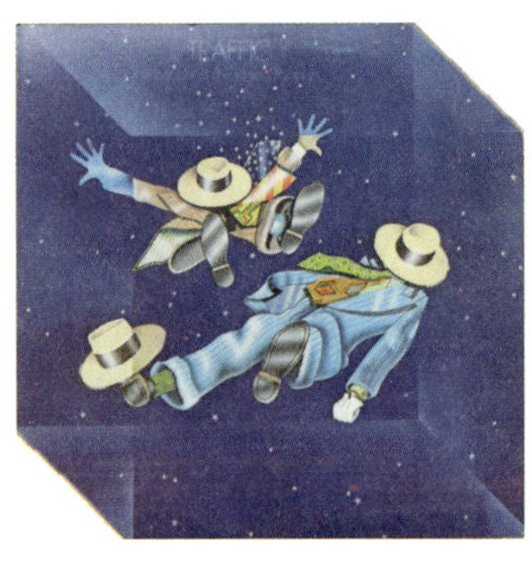

TRAFFIC
"(SOMETIMES I FEEL SO) UNINSPIRED"

Island LP ILPS 9224—1973
Writers: Steve Winwood and Jim Capaldi

Traffic's Jim Capaldi recorded at Muscle Shoals Sound toward the end of 1971. He came back to England raving about the studio's rhythm section and convinced the other members of Traffic to hire musicians David Hood and Roger Hawkins to join Traffic for their 1972 American tour. Traffic came to Muscle Shoals Sound that December to record their sixth album, *Shoot Out at the Fantasy Factory*. The track "(Sometimes I Feel So) Uninspired" finds Steve Winwood delivering a guitar solo that transcends his blues roots.

PAUL SIMON
"KODACHROME"

Columbia 4-45859—1973
Writer: Paul Simon

In 1972, Paul Simon fell in love with the Staple Singers' singles cut at Muscle Shoals Sound and planned to record just one song, "Take Me to the Mardi Gras," at the studio. To his astonishment, the Rhythm Section cut a perfect master in one or two takes. He was only thirty minutes into the first of six sessions he had paid for. He then began to play half-finished songs, asking the Rhythm Section which ones they wanted to cut. The first song they attempted was called "Going Home," which evolved into "Kodachrome." Released as a single in 1973, "Kodachrome" reached #2 on the pop charts.

BOB SEGER
"OLD TIME ROCK & ROLL"

Capitol 4702—1979
Writers: George Jackson and Thomas E. Jones

"Old Time Rock & Roll" was written by Memphis songwriter George Jackson with a friend, Tom Jones III. Jimmy Johnson thought that if they overdubbed Jackson Highway singer Dennis Gulley on Jackson's demo it might make "Old Time Rock & Roll" more attractive to prospective rock & roll clients. As soon as Gulley sang it, Johnson and David Hood both thought it was perfect for Bob Seger. The Detroit rocker tried to cut the song with both his Silver Bullet Band and the Swampers, but he eventually just overdubbed his vocal on George Jackson's demo.

HANK WILLIAMS JR.
"FAMILY TRADITION"

Elektra E-460646-A—1979
Writer: Hank Williams Jr.

With his 1975 album *Hank Williams Jr. and Friends*, recorded at Music Mill Studios in Muscle Shoals, the son of Hank Williams reinvented himself, moving away from the countrypolitan sound and becoming part of the Outlaw movement. In 1979, Williams recorded *Family Tradition* at both Wishbone studio in Muscle Shoals and in Nashville for Elektra/Curb. The album reached the Top Five on the country charts. The title cut reached #4 on the country charts.

SHENANDOAH
"TWO DOZEN ROSES"

Columbia 69061—1989
Writers: Robert Byrne and Mac McAnally

In 1987, songwriter Robert Byrne and Rick Hall started recording a Muscle Shoals band from a bar just down the street from the FAME studio. Over the next three years, Hall and Byrne produced three albums on Shenandoah for Columbia Records, from which an impressive ten singles reached the country Top Ten, four of which went #1. "Two Dozen Roses" was taken from the second Shenandoah album produced by Hall and Byrne, entitled *The Road Not Taken*.

CONTRIBUTORS

JASON ISBELL is a singer, songwriter, guitarist, and bandleader from Green Hill, Alabama, who has won six Grammys and nine Americana Music awards as a solo artist and with his band, the 500 Unit. He got his first music publishing deal with FAME in Muscle Shoals and is a former member of the Drive-By Truckers.

RJ SMITH is a Writer-Editor at the Country Music Hall of Fame and Museum. He is the author of books on Chuck Berry, James Brown, Robert Frank, and Black Los Angeles in the 1940s. His work has also appeared in the *Village Voice*, *The New York Times*, and *Maggot Brain*.

PATTERSON HOOD is a musician and songwriter based in Portland, Oregon. He grew up in Muscle Shoals and co-founded the band Drive-By Truckers with Mike Cooley. He works as a solo artist and also continues to play in the Drive-By Truckers.

WARREN DENNEY is Vice President for Creative at the Country Music Hall of Fame and Museum. He has written for *Nashville Musician*, *The East Nashvillian*, and other publications.

MICHAEL A. GONZALES is a music journalist, essayist, and short story writer who has written for the *Village Voice*, *Wax Poetics*, *Essence*, *The Wire UK*, and *Spin*. He currently contributes to CrimeReads.com, Oldster.com, MemoirLand.com, and Open Secrets.com.

FRANCESCA T. ROYSTER is Professor of English at DePaul University in Chicago. Her books include *Black Country Music: Listening for Revolutions* and *Choosing Family: A Memoir of Queer Motherhood and Black Resistance*.

STEPHEN DEUSNER is a critic and historian whose writing has appeared in *Uncut*, *Pitchfork*, *The New York Times*, and *The Washington Post*. He is the author of *Where the Devil Don't Stay: Traveling the South with the Drive-By Truckers* and the album study *Garth Brooks in… The Life of Chris Gaines*.

ERICKA BLOUNT is an award-winning journalist, author, screenwriter, producer, and professor. She's currently a full-time lecturer at the Cathy Hughes School of Communications at Howard University.

MARLIN GREENE has composed, recorded, engineered, and produced music in Muscle Shoals and elsewhere. Among the artists he has worked with are Leon Russell, Boz Scaggs, Joe Tex, Solomon Burke, Eddie Hinton, and R.B. Greaves.

ROB BOWMAN is the author of numerous lines notes and several books, including *Soulsville USA: The Story of Stax Records*, *The Last Soul Company: The Malaco Records Story*, and, most recently, *Land of a Thousand Sessions: The Complete Muscle Shoals Story, 1951–1985*.

This 1970 Fender Rosewood Telecaster belonged to Pops Staples of the Staple Singers.
He played it when the group performed "The Weight" with the Band in *The Last Waltz*, the 1978 concert film directed by Martin Scorsese.

GIFT OF MARTY STUART, WILLARD AND PAT WALKER CHARITABLE FOUNDATION, AND LORETTA AND JEFF CLARKE. FROM THE MARTY STUART COLLECTION

2025 BOARD OF OFFICERS AND TRUSTEES

CIRCLE GUARD

The Country Music Hall of Fame and Museum Circle Guard unites and celebrates individuals who have given their time, talent, and treasure to safeguard the integrity of country music and make it accessible to a global audience through the Museum. The Circle Guard designation ranks as the grandest distinction afforded to those whose unwavering commitment to the Museum protects the legacies of the members of the Country Music Hall of Fame, and, by extension, the time-honored achievements of all who are part of the country music story.

Steve Turner, Founder (1947– 2025)

Kyle Young, Commander General

David Conrad

Bill Denny

Ken Levitan

Mary Ann McCready

Mike Milom

Jay Orr

Ken Roberts (1932 – 2022)

Seab Tuck

Jerry B. Williams

Jody Williams

Welcome To
CITY of MUSCLE SHOALS
Hit RECORDING
CAPITAL of the World